CLASSIC WARPLANES

REPUBLIC F-105 THUNDERCHIEF

Doug Richardson

SMITHMARK

A SALAMANDER BOOK

©Salamander Books Ltd. 1992
129-137 York Way,
London N7 9LG,
United Kingdom.

ISBN 0-8317-1410-7

This edition published in 1992 by
SMITHMARK Publishers, Inc., 112
Madison Avenue, New York, NY 10016.

SMITHMARK Books are available for
bulk purchase for sales promotion and
premium use. For details write or
telephone the Manager of Special Sales,
SMITHMARK Publishers, Inc., 112
Madison Avenue, New York, NY 10016.
(212) 532-6660.

CREDITS

Editor: Chris Westhorp
Designer: Philip Gorton
Color artwork: ©Pilot Press Ltd and
Salamander Books Ltd.
Three-view, side-view and cutaway
drawings: ©Pilot Press Ltd.
Filmset by The Old Mill, London
Color reproduction by Graham Curtis
Repro, England
Printed in Belgium by Proost International
Book Production, Turnhout.

ACKNOWLEDGEMENTS

The publishers would like to thank
Robert F. Dorr for his photographic
contribution to this work.

AUTHOR

DOUG RICHARDSON is a defence journalist and author specializing in the fields of aviation, guided missiles and electronics. After a successful career as an electronics and aerospace engineer he moved into journalism. He has been the Defence Editor of "Flight International", Editor of "Military Technology", and Editor of "Defense Materiel" before becoming a full-time freelance writer.

He has written many Salamander Books including "The Illustrated Guide to Electronic Warfare", "The F-16 Fact File", "The AH-1 Fact File", An Illustrated Survey of the West's Modern Fighters" and "Stealth Warplanes".

CONTENTS

IN January 1951, the United States Air Force (USAF) issued a document defining the military characteristics of the planned replacement for the Republic F-84F fighter-bomber. Standard fighter-bombers of the time were the straight-winged Republic F-84D, -84E and -84G Thunderjet. Tough and rugged, these had been built in large numbers (154, 743, and 789 respectively), and 335 of them were lost in combat in the Korean War. The swept-wing F-84F Thunderstreak, which the Long Island-based Republic company were preparing for its first flight, was hoped to win the resulting contract.

Yet to fly, the F-84F Thunderstreak (originally designated the F-96) was a swept-wing fighter based on the older aircraft. Expected to be a low-cost adaption which would use 55 per cent of the existing tooling, it was due to be delivered to the USAF from early 1952 onwards.

POWERPLANT

A key part of the new requirement was the need for an internal weapons bay able to carry a nuclear weapon, so Republic's initial studies for a "Super F-84F" looked at what was essentially a scaled-up version of the existing aircraft. One problem was the choice of powerplant. The straight-winged F-84 series had used various versions of the Allison J35 turbojet, starting with the 4,000lb (1,814kg) J35-A-15.

For the swept-wing F-84F the 5,300lb (2,404kg) J35-A-25 was chosen, but flight trials soon showed that the aircraft was underpowered. It was re-engined with the 7,220lb (3,275kg) Wright J65, a licence-built version of the British Armstrong Siddeley Sap-

phire, but this engine's subsequent history of problems ensured that a new powerplant would be used for the next fighter-bomber, even if more powerful Sapphire variants could be offered.

Initially, Republic opted for the General Electric J73, the engine developed for the F-86H version of the Sabre. As alternatives, the company briefly looked at the Alison J71 used on the B-66 Skywarrior, the Wright J67 (a licence-built version of another British engine, the Bristol Olympus), and Pratt & Whitney's new two-spool J57, the engine being developed in dry form for the B-52 and, with afterburning, for the F-100.

In April 1952 Republic offered Model AP-63 to the USAF. Essentially a scaled up F-84F, this would be powered by the J71. Development was approved in the following month, even though no formal requirement existed. The January 1951 outline specification had been revised in January 1952, but the USAF had yet to commit itself to a formal requirement. The contract issued in September 1952 called for the first of a planned fleet of 199 aircraft to be ready for service in 1955, an ambitious schedule which would prove impossible to meet.

ENGINE PROBLEMS

March 1953 saw the programme cut back to only 37 of these F-105 fighters plus nine examples of the proposed RF-105 reconnaissance model. An armistice ended the Korean War that summer, taking some of the urgency out of the entire project.

Mock-up inspection took place in October and no large-scale changes to the proposed design were required. By now it had become obvious that, in its

current form, the J71 engine would not have enough thrust for the new fighter. Use of the J57 as an interim powerplant was discussed, with the idea that once the J71 was delivering sufficient thrust production could be switched back to this engine. It was clear that the proposed operational date of 1955 was totally unrealistic, so in December the USAF suspended the planned procurement and effectively cancelled the programme.

Procurement was reinstated in February 1954, and the decision was taken to use Pratt & Whitney's J57 as an interim engine for the initial prototypes. Production aircraft would have the same company's J75, a scaled-up version of the J57 which would see civil service as the JT4 on Boeing 707 and Douglas DC-8 airliners. Fitted with an afterburner, this massive two-spool engine would deliver more than 10 tons of thrust. February also saw mock-up inspection of the RF-105; but in September came a cutback to only three prototypes, a number soon doubled to six in the following month.

OFFICIAL GO-AHEAD

In December 1954, the Pentagon finally published GOR 49, the official requirement for the new fighter-bomber. Updated three times over the ensuing few months, it allowed the USAF to authorize a total of 15 test aircraft — two F-105As, 10 F-105Bs, plus three RF-105s. GOR 49 specified a heavy

Right: Silence reigns briefly between shifts at Republic's Long Island production line. Cook-Carnegie planning ensured a speedy build-up of deliveries.

fighter-bomber carrying an advanced fire-control system, and facilities for airborne refuelling. In practice, it was written to match the aircraft taking shape on Republic's drawing boards.

Such was the pace of aviation technology at the time, that the new aircraft was expected to serve "from 1958 through 1960." The idea of building a new warplane with an operational lifetime of only three years would have been rejected a decade later, let alone today, but these were the days of the Cold War when the growing strength of the Soviet Union called for urgent action.

CONSTRUCTION

The new fighter would be the USAF's first custom-designed fighter-bomber, and the first US fighter to be developed under the weapon system concept. Today, the concept of making a single contractor responsible for the entire programme in all its aspects is normal, but for the time it was considered unusual.

Another innovation was the Cook-Carnegie production plan. This called for the test aircraft to be built not in the experimental shop in the traditional manner, but on the production line using production drawings and tooling. While the assembly line was still moving at low pace, intensive flight testing was expected to identify any changes needed. The resulting modifications would be made to the drawings and tooling so that these could be incorporated within early production aircraft.

History and Development

If all went well, the Cook-Carnegie scheme promised to speed up the programme. Should an aircraft bog down in technical problems, however, the revisions to the tools and drawings would be late, causing early production aircraft to reflect the problems of the flight-test fleet. The Convair F-102 was to fall victim to exactly such a process in late 1953 with two-thirds of the tools purchased under the Cook-Carnegie plan having to be scrapped and new ones bought.

For the structure of the new warplane, Republic adopted two techniques not in common use at the time. One was the use of forgings in areas of high stress; the other was the use of machine milling to vary the thickness of skin panels, leaving metal thick in areas of high stress and shaving it away to a greater or lesser degree in areas where less strength was needed.

The original AP-63 proposals had featured a mid-set wing and a horizontal stabiliser set about a quarter way up the vetical fin. In refining this basic layout, Republic took advantage of the latest research into supersonic flight carried out by the US National Advisory Committee on Aeronautics (NACA). Longitudinal stability had been a problem in several "Century series" fighters, and NACA recommended that this be avoided by mounting the all-moving horizontal tail surfaces as low as possible on the fuselage and mounting the wing relatively high. (The UK had adopted the same approach with equal success earlier in the decade with its English Electric P1.)

DISASTER

Long Island was too congested a location for flight testing a supersonic

Below: Russell Roth test-flies the short-lived first YF-105A. The aircraft was powered by a Pratt & Whitney J57 turbojet fed by simple elliptical air inlets.

fighter, so the first two YF-105 prototypes were shipped to Edwards Air Force Base (AFB), where 54-0098 made its maiden flight on 22 October 1955 in the hands of Republic's chief test pilot, Russell ''Rusty'' Roth. Closer in appearance to the eventual production aircraft than the F-84F-style configuration first offered to the USAF in April 1952, it did retain one feature from the Thunderstreak: its J57-P-25 engine was fed by simple inlets of elliptical form.

By this stage, Republic was under no doubt that considerable redesign would be needed to create the production version. Although the YF-105 had gone supersonic during the 45-minute maiden flight, the design's supersonic capability was minimal. Not only was it underpowered with the interim engine, its fuselage did not take into account the recently-discovered ''Area Rule'', a method of shaping the aircraft which minimized supersonic drag considerably.

On 16 December, Roth was flying a 5.5g turn at the end of a high speed run when the starboard mainlanding gear suddenly extended. It was promptly torn off by the 530kt slipstream. Roth elected to fly the damaged aircraft back to Edwards AFB and attempt to land using only the port main gear and nosewheel. The nose hit the runway hard enough to break the back of the aircraft. With only 22 flying hours on its airframe, it was returned to Republic — officially for repair — but never flew again. Roth resumed flight testing on 28 January 1956 using 54-0099, the second prototype. Unrepresenative of the planned production configuration, it had a short career. All the attention was now focussed on the much-modified F-105B, which was taking shape at Long Island.

Below: The second YF-105A acts as tanker for the third YF-105B. Note the smaller vertical fin on the older aircraft. 40099 was soon retired from development flying.

TURNING the YF-105A into the true supersonic fighter was a job which had started well before the YF-105As had flown. It involved installing the definitive Pratt & Whitney J75 engine, redesigning the fuselage according to the drag-reducing Area Rule principle devised by Richard T. Whitcomb of the US National Advisory Committee on Aeronautics (NACA), installing new inlets better suited to flight at high supersonic speeds, increasing the directional stability by raising the height and increasing the area of the vertical fin, strengthening the horizontal tail surfaces to avoid a flutter problem which had torn the tail from two wind tunnel models, and installing the avoinics needed for the strike mission.

Many of these changes were similar to those incorporated in other "Century series" warplanes. For example, area ruling was also added to Convair's YF-102A in 1954/55 in order to provide a supersonic capability; while 1954 saw the tail of the F-100A increased in height to improve stability.

INLET DESIGN

The new inlet was of a novel configuration and was based on that planned for the F-103 (Republic's planned Mach 3 fighter). Given that the company was trying to coax Mach 2 performance out of the successor to the barely-supersonic YF-105A, the idea of a parallel project to build a huge titanium Mach 3 fighter may seem unbelievable, but aircraft designers (and the Pentagon) thought boldly in the mid-1950s. The F-103 was cancelled in September 1957, but not before engineers conceived the idea of taking the basic inlet design, complete

with its forward sloped leading edge, turning it through 90deg, scaling it down to size, and applying it to the Mach 2 F-105B.

WING DESIGN

Variable geometry was needed to match the airflow to the engine's demands over the full speed range, so a system of moveable contoured plugs was used to vary the inlet capture area. Air-bleed doors were fitted to the fuselage, but designers rejected the concept of mounting suck-in doors on the sides of the inlet (the normal method of supplying extra air to the engine during take-off). Instead, a set of auxiliary doors operating only when the undercarriage was lowered allowed the engine to draw the extra air it needed from the wheel wells.

It was a neat solution, but one which contained an unforeseen design flaw: wing leading-edge sweepback angle was 45deg; thickness ratio was 5.3 per cent at the root, falling to 3.7 per cent at the tip; wing area was only 385ft^2 (35.77m^2); and since typical take-off weight would be in the order of 45,000lb (20,412 kg), wing loading would be high.

To maximize lift, the wing would have full-span leading-edge slats, plus trailing-edge "Fowler" flaps of partial span. For take-off and landing, both were set to their maximum deflections of 20 and 34.5deg respectively. For subsonic cruise and manoeuvring, the flaps were kept raised, but with the slats positioned at 8deg.

Roll control was by means of short-span outboard ailerons, plus upper surface spoilers. At high supersonic speeds, the ailerons were locked out to avoid possible problems due to wing

twisting. Pitch control was by means of a low-set all-moving horizontal tail. Ailerons and stabilizer were fully powered by hydraulics, each having two primary systems. An emergency system powered by an automatically-extending ram-air turbine was also provided.

THE J75 TURBOFAN

Pratt & Whitney's J75 was a good choice of powerplant. Although there was no truth in the hoary old joke that you could throw a brick down the inlet of an F-105 and watch it emerge from the afterburner as a puff of sand, this big turbojet was tough. Free of the foibles from which the first-generations of afterburning turbofans would suffer, it had some reliability problems in service but coped with the demands of jet combat, including massive use of afterburner.

The eight-stage, low-pressure (LP) compressor led to a seven-stage, high-

Left: This head-on view of a YF-105B at Edwards AFB shows the instrumented mast and the novel forward-swept air inlets devised for supersonic flight.

pressure (HP) compressor. From here the air entered an eight-unit, can-annular combustor whose efflux passed through a single-stage HP turbine and then a two-stage LP turbine. Running at full military (dry) power, the J75-P-19W, which powered the majority of production aircraft, swallowed 220lb (100kg) of fuel/min, equivalent to 0.5gal/sec (1.9l). Turn on the massive afterburner and the thrust rose from 16,000lb (7,303kg) to 24,500lb (11,113kg). With more than 2gal (7.6l) of fuel now being burned every second, the fuel gauge spiralled downward at 972lb/min (441kg). Internal fuel capacity was 1,135USgal, all carried in three fuselage tanks: 376gal in the forward tank, 257gal in the main tank, and 502gal in the aft tank.

Right: Wrapped around the jetpipe of the massive J75 turbojet was Thunderchief's other novel feature — a four-section airbrake which also acted as a variable nozzle.

Above: Republic's F-105 was probably the last fighter designed by engineers determined to create an aircraft which would combine performance with visual beauty.

The "W" suffix in the engine designation indicates water-injection. When maximum power was needed, a spray ring added demineralized water to the air entering the compressor. This cooled the air and boosted the maximum thrust to 26,500lb (12,020kg) at sea-level.

Wrapped around the jetpipe was one of the aircraft's unique features: a four-segment nozzle. This had two operating positions. Normally the four segments formed a smoothly contoured rear end to the fuselage, but when afterburner was selected they opened by 9deg to create a larger nozzle. It was far from the sophistication of today's continuously-variable nozzles, but it worked well enough. All four segments could be opened wide in the air to act as airbrakes, but with the undercarriage lowered only the side segments could operate in this manner.

THE F-105B

Heart of the new avionics suite was General Electric's MA-8 fire-control system. This included an E-34 ranging radar, E-30 toss-bombing computer, E-50 gyro-computing sighting system, and a T-145 weapons system to handle "special stores" — better known as nuclear weapons.

The end result of all these modifications was the F-105B. In March 1956, even before the redesigned fighter had flown, 10 million US Dollars was allocated to allow work to start on the planned procurement of 65 F-105Bs

Thud Technology

Above: This view of the second YF-105B at Edwards AFB shows the small rear-view windows aft of the main canopy. These were deleted on production aircraft.

and 17 RF-105s. The first flight of 54-0100, the prototype F-105B, took place on 26 May 1956, with test pilot Henry Beaird at the controls. All went well until Beaird lowered the undercarriage in preparation for landing whereupon the nose wheel refused to budge. After cycling the gear several times, the pilot retracted the main undercarriage and belly-landed the aircraft on the dry lake. The fuselage cracked; some reports attribute this was due to the shock of landing, but others claim that the aircraft was dropped while being recovered by crane.

Despite this setback, June saw five F-105C added to the programme. This new version was to be a two-seat trainer. In July, the USAF decided to cancel the RF-105 programme. The three aircraft under construction were too far along to be completed as B models, so were reclassified as JF-105B, with the "J" prefix indicating special test aircraft. The first would fly on 18 July, and all three were assigned to various F-105 trials.

EVALUATIONS

Since the days of the propellor-driven P-47 Thunderbolt, Republic aircraft names had maintained a "Thunder" series. Following a company-wide competition to name the new fighter, in June 1956 it suggested "Thunderchief", a name approved by the USAF in the following month.

Category II testing of the new warplane started on 8 January 1957, but the aircraft being evaluated in this joint Republic/USAF effort was far from the eventual production standard. Many of the aircraft's systems required additional testing, which often threw up the need for time-consuming modifications, while other changes were introduced by the customer. On 22 January 1957, the USAF ordered that all new tactical aircraft be fitted with the APN-105 all-weather navigation system. This involved a major pre-production modification to the F-105.

On 30 January the company test pilot, Lindell Hendrix, found himself flying another Thunderchief with undercarriage problems. Coming in to land in the second F-105B, he found himself unable to lower the main undercarriage. On the first F-105B it

was the nosewheel which had stuck; now, on the second, it was the main gear which remained firmly raised. Once again, it was belly-landing time. Hendrix brought the aircraft down safely, climbed out, and was rewarded a few moments later by the sight of the main gear slowly lowering!

An investigation finally assigned the blame to that novel auxiliary inlet in the wheel wells: the auxiliary inlet door had opened accidentally, allowing the engine to try to draw air from the wheel well; when Hendrix tried to lower the undercarriage, the resulting suction had been more than enough to keep the doors firmly shut against the combined forces of gravity and the undercarriage actuation system. A mechanical interlock was hurriedly devised to ensure that in future the auxiliary inlet door would remain shut as long as the undercarriage was retracted.

ALL-WEATHER STRIKE

That summer saw a major revision of GOR 49. The F-105B promised to be an adequate day bomber, but what the USAF really wanted was an all-weather strike aircraft. Republic was asked to submit proposals for an advanced version of the F-105. When reissued on 2 November, GOR 49 formalized the use of the APN-105 in place of the inertial navigation system originally planned; specified full all-weather attack capability; defined a new cockpit instrument display; and added a requirement that the aircraft be able to carry and deliver the TX-43 nuclear weapon.

By the middle of the year the USAF had approved the cockpit mock-up of the all-weather F-105D model. Destined to be the definitive single-seat model, this would have an improved cockpit with vertical instruments; a redesigned nose fitted with a large radome and packed full of the avionics needed for the revised mission; plus an uprated engine incorporating water injection. Development of a recce model was also reinstated, this time based on the new F-105D, but 1957 also saw cancellation of the F-105C two-seater.

INTO PRODUCTION

By April 1958 all test aircraft had been built and work was under way on the first production model of the F-105B. Handover of the first aircraft took place on 27 May and the F-105B Thunderchief officially entered operational service in August 1958, the first unit being the 335th Tactical Fighter Squadron of Tactical Air Command's (TAC) 4th Fighter Wing. At first, this unit was based at Eglin AFB where it carried out operational tests of the aircraft. (Later it would move to Seymour-Johnson AFB.)

Below: Braking parachute deployed, 54-0102 — the third of four YF-105B development aircraft — taxies in after one of its first test flights at Edwards AFB.

To describe the F-105 as being in operational service was little more than a public relations exercise. Rockwell were still having problems in meeting the proposed schedule, and TAC would not have its first full-strength F-105B squadron until the summer of the following year. In November, in an attempt to catch up with the many modifications which were due to be made to production aircraft, Republic

Above: Aircraft 54-0104 — seen here on an early test flight — was the first of five F105B-5RE Thunderchiefs built to serve as evaluation and test examples.

took the drastic step of stopping the production line.

A USAF investigation showed that part of the problem was that the customer and contractor were still unfamiliar with the weapon system concept, while the Cook-Carnegie production schedule was resulting in the delivery of early production aircraft which lacked the capability of those which followed. Company management was also criticised for having virtually lost control of the programme and being slow to recognize emerging problems.

Management weakness was to remain a problem over the next two decades. Renamed Fairchild, the company had problems in manufacturing the A-10 in the 1970s, and would be driven out of the military aircraft business in the 1980s with the cancellation of the T-46 trainer.

By now the reader might be excused in thinking that the Thunderchief was set to be a failure. Production may have been painfully slow, modifications

Thud Technology

frequent, reliability low, and maintenance demands high, but once airborne the new fighter handled well. It was free from the handling problems which plagued many of its contemporaries, and could even be flown safely over most of the performance envelope with the stability augmentation system turned off. Like the F-111 a decade later the early production aircraft wasn't quite what TAC really wanted, but was very much better than anything they currently had. It slowly won the respect of its crews.

As a follow-on to the F-105B, the USAF had settled for a four-year schedule under which it would take delivery of 472 aircraft, a mix of F-105D single seaters and F-105E two-seaters. Republic soon found that the F-105D timescale was as prone to slippage as that of the F-105B, and was forced to request repeated revisions to the production schedule.

It had been hoped to build D models on the same production line as the B, but the changes to the airframe made the D virtually an all-new aircraft. For example, the new engine

Above: Nine different versions of the F-105D were developed. This is one of 121 F-105D-10REs, the first version to be built in three-figure numbers.

required changes of the fuselage and intake ducts, while the increased all-up weight involved a stronger main undercarriage and improved brakes. Assembly of each F-105D would take 214 working days rather than the 144 needed for each B model.

Throughout 1958 work continued on the planned recce derivative. Designed to carry cameras, infra-red (IR) sensors, and a pod-mounted sideways-looking radar (SLR), this would also carry the equipment needed to develop films in flight, ejecting the processed film cassette for recovery by the ground forces which needed the imagery. The project proved short-lived. Two days before Christmas, it was cancelled. The formal requirement (SOR-49-2) remained valid until April 1962, when the revised SOR-192 was released to set in motion the RF-4C programme.

In January 1959, the F-105B was finally declared operational — largely an exercise in window-dressing, for in practice the new aircraft was far from combat ready. The 335th TFS was being used as a test unit, but even so would not have its full quota of 18 aircraft until the summer. July saw the arrival of the first four F-105Bs at what would become the first true operational Thunderchief squadron — the 334th TFS. Despite the fact that its pilots all had a minimum of 200 hours in "Century-series" fighters, working up on the new fighter took a year. Absence of a two-seater meant that trainees had to make their first flight on the type after ground training only.

Initial production aircraft were designated F-105B-10 and fitted with the J75-P-5 engine, as was the generally-similar F-105B-15 model. First flown in June 1959, the F-15B-20 featured modified avionics plus the J75-P-19, a modified engine offering an extra 1,000lb (454kg) of thrust. This engine was later retrofitted to earlier aircraft. Another retrofit scheme added a Goodyear anti-skid braking system.

F-105D INTO SERVICE

Production of the F-105E was cancelled on 29 March 1959. The USAF had two reasons for doing this; the F-105E was more expensive than the D, while reducing procurement to a single model would allow Republic to focus all its energies on the F-105D.

This was a very different aircraft to the F-105B. Externally, the most obvious change was the installation of a much larger nose radome. The tiny radome at the extreme nose of the

Right: The F-105D-5RE was the first D version to be built in production quantity. Only three of the earlier F-105D-1REs were made, and used for testing.

Above: An F-105B-15RE of the 33rd TFS is caught by the camera in November 1960 as it cruises in clean condition. Note the Indian-head logo beneath the cockpit.

F-105B had covered the small and relatively-simple E-34 ranging radar, part of General Electric's MA-8 fire-control system. The larger radome on the F-105D covered a more sophisticated radar set. Developed by the Autonetics division of North American Aviation, the NASARR R-14A X-band radar offered air-to-air and air-to-ground modes, combining search and ranging functions. Along

with the APN-105 Doppler radar first used on the F-105B, it formed part of the ASG-19 Thunderstick fire-control system.

Within the cockpit, the traditional circular-dial instruments used on other contemporary fighters had been replaced by the latest concept in display technology — vertical tape instruments in which key information was shown in the form of vertical bars whose variable height could be read against vertical scales. Preset values which had to be maintained, for example when flying an instrument landing, could be set on the vertical scale, leaving the pilot with the task of keeping the various bars aligned with the reference markers.

Another important change was the installation of the most powerful version of the J75 currently available. The J75-P-19W had the same 24,500lb maximum afterburning thrust as the -19 engine used in the F-105B. For take-off, the newer engine used water injection temporarily to boost the thrust to 26,500lb (12,020kg).

First flight of 58-1146, the first F-105D, took place on 9 June, a month ahead of time, with Lindell Hendrix at the controls. All went well, with no hint of the problems which had

Above: On the F-105D, vertical tape instruments replaced many of the traditional round-dial gauges. By the standards of 1959, this was advanced technology.

Below: A heavily-loaded F-105D-5RE carries live bombs on the wing pylons, and on the fuselage centreline. Maximum warload was around six tons.

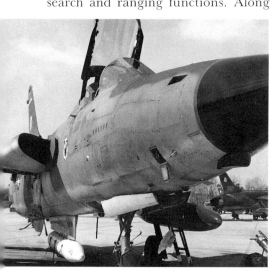

Thud Technology

dogged the YF-105A and F-105B prototypes. Wringing out the bugs in such a complex aircraft would obviously take time, but at last the USAF had the aircraft it really wanted — a Thunderchief which combined superb handling qualities with all-weather strike capability.

What the USAF did baulk at was the cost. A commission was convened to see what could be done to save money by simplifying the aircraft. It was a short-sighted decision. The commission voted to delete all the aircraft's EW systems: the radar-warning receiver, radar jammer, and chaff dispensers; the fuel-tank fire detection/suppression system; and even the 0.8in (20mm) M61 cannon. The cannon was eventually retained, but the other "cost savings" were to prove costly in lives and aircraft when the Thunderchief finally saw combat.

Meanwhile, production of the simpler F-105B ended in December 1959 with the delivery of a batch of six aircraft, the last of a total of 75 purchased at an average flyway cost of 5.6 million US Dollars. On 11 December, an F-105B set a new world speed record for a 100km closed course, its speed of 1,056kt breaking the previous record of 955kt established that summer by the Nord Griffon II.

Production of the F-105B might have ended, but the aircraft had yet to complete formal testing. Category II testing should have ended in November 1959, but did not officially end until 30 March 1960. Even then, some Category II tests had to be slipped beyond that date when testing uncovered problems with the MA-8 fire-control system, autopilot, and central air data computer. Until the bugs were wrung out of the aircraft and its systems, it was near-useless as an operational aircraft. During the first three months of 1960, none of the 56 F-105Bs in TAC service was operationally ready.

Above: In the early stages of the Vietnam War, some aicraft remained uncamouflaged. These F-105Ds were operating from Takhli, Thailand, in April 1966.

Right: An F-105D-5RE of the 357th TFS (tailcode RU) leads an -5RE (centre) and a -15RE (foreground) of the 44th TFS (tailcode RE) during a 1970 mission.

Category III testing had to await the completion of Project Optimize, a scheme which incorporated 26 engineering changes intended to eliminate most of the problems. Due to be completed by April 1960, this slipped several months.

The additional Category II tests had been completed in the summer of 1960, allowing third-stage testing to begin in July. Two squadrons were available for this work: the 335th (now at Nellis AFB) and the 334th at Williams AFB, Arizona. Despite problems due to shortage of spares, Category III testing was completed on 15 August and the low reliability of the MA-8 promised troubles to come.

Similar problems plagued the new F-105D. Category I testing was hampered by speed restrictions and problems with the new engine. Category II tests could not start in May 1960 as had been planned, slipping to December due to production delays and aircraft modifications. Once again the 335th TFS found itself

testing a new fighter. With the new powerplant proven in Category I testing, as well as on the F-105B, attention could be focussed on the new avionics and cockpit instrumentation. Category II testing ended in October 1961 and was followed by Category III tests at Seymour-Johnson AFB — a location rapidly becoming the centre of TAC's F-105 expertise.

Formal acceptance by TAC of its first F-105D took place at Nellis AFB on 28 September 1960. The new variant was declared operational with TAC's 4th Fighter Wing in 1961.

Throughout 1961, the reliability of the F-105B remained low, as the USAF struggled in the face of spares shortages and lack of maintenance skills. Around 150 man hours of maintenance was needed for every flying hour, and temporary groundings were frequent.

Early experience with the D model proved happier, although all were temporarily grounded in December 1961 following the failure of a main fuselage

the aircraft and deliveries to the PACAF would not begin until October. On 18 June, a Taft-Hartley legal injunction ended the strike at Republic, but the same month saw yet another grounding of the F-105B and D following two accidents at Nellis AFB. An investigation highlighted problems with chafing and flight control deficiencies. The USAF launched Project Look Alike. As its name suggests, this would not only clear many of the reliability problems, but would also remove the differences between the individual production batches, bringing all F-105Ds to the -25RE production standard. On the oldest aircraft it involved some 385 individual modifications.

Look Alike added some new features, giving all aircraft the ability to carry up to 16,750lb (7,598kg) of bombs, and to launch Bullpup missiles. The skin was also sealed with a lacquer which prevented moisture from entering the fuselage and avionics units.

From the relatively simple programme first envisaged, this soon

frame during fatigue testing at Wright-Patterson AFB. Even when cracked, the frame was found to have considerable strength; here was the first evidence of the structural toughness which would keep battle-damaged Thuds flying over the skies of North Vietnam later in the decade. Republic engineers hastily devised the tooling needed to strengthen the frame.

In May 1961 came the first deployment to Europe. The USAFE would eventually deploy two Thunderchief wings in West Germany: the 36th TFW at Bitburg, and the 49th at Spangdahlem. Frequent training deployments were made from Germany to Wheelus AB in Libya. The Republic aircraft would serve in Europe until 1966.

PROJECT LOOK ALIKE

Further disruption to the USAF's Thunderchief deployment plans came in April 1962 when a strike began at Republic. This delayed deployment of

Below: An F-105D-25RE flies with a heavy ordnance load. Only 80 were built, but Project Look Alike modified most older aircraft to the -25RE build standard.

Thud Technology

Republic F-105D Thunderchief cutaway drawing key

1 Pitot tube
2 Radome
3 Radar scanner dish
4 Radar mounting and tracking mechanism
5 Forward electronic counter-measures (ECM) antenna
6 Aft-facing strike camera
7 Radome hinge
8 ADF sense aerial
9 Fire control radar transmitter/receiver
10 Cannon muzzle
11 Instrument electronics
12 In-flight refuelling position light
13 Air refuelling receptacle
14 Cannon ammunition drum (1,028 rounds)
15 Liquid oxygen converter
16 Angle of attack transmitter
17 Cannon barrels
18 Nosewheel doors
19 M-61 20mm six-barrel rotary cannon
20 Ammunition feel chute
21 Gun gas venting pipe
22 Air refuelling probe housing
23 Alternator and electrical bay
24 Air driven turbine
25 Air refuelling probe
26 Windshield rain dispersal duct
27 Bullet proof windscreen panels
28 Radar attack sight
29 Instrument panel shroud
30 Navigation radar display
31 Rudder pedals
32 Cockpit front pressure bulkhead
33 Cannon mounting
34 Nosewheel leg strut
35 ILS system radar reflector
36 Taxying lamps
37 Nosewheel
38 Torque scissor links
39 Hydraulic steering controls
40 Flight control system hydraulics bay
41 Electronics cooling air outlet
42 IFF aerial
43 UHF aerial
44 Underfloor radio and electronics bay
45 Cockpit pressure floor level
46 Pilot's side console panel
47 Engine throttle
48 Control column
49 Pilot's ejection seat
50 Seat back parachute pack
51 Headrest
52 Cockpit canopy cover
53 3,000lb (1,360kg) HE bomb (inboard pylon)
54 Starboard air intake
55 Cockpit canopy jack
56 Canopy hinge
57 Air conditioning pack

58 Cockpit rear pressure bulkhead
59 Secondary electronics bay
60 Air data computer
61 Port air intake
62 Bomb bay fuel tank, 325 Imp gal (1 477 l)
63 Boundary layer splitter plate
64 Intake duct variable area sliding ramp
65 Forward group of fuselage fuel tanks: total internal fuel capacity 966 Imp gal (4390 l)
66 Gyro compass platform
67 Bomb bay fuel tank fuel transfer lines
68 Fuselage/front spar main frame
69 Dorsal spine fairing
70 Starboard mainwheel, stowed position
71 375 Imp gal (1 705 l) external fuel tank
72 AIM-9 Sidewinder air-to-air missile
73 Missile launcher rail
74 Twin missile carrier (outboard pylon)
75 Starboard leading edge flap
76 Outboard pylon fixing/drop tank filler cap
77 Starboard navigation light
78 Static dischargers
79 Starboard aileron
80 Starboard fowler lap
81 Trim tab, starboard only
82 Flap guide rails
83 Roll control spoilers
84 Anti-collision light
85 Air intake ducting
86 Ground running secondary air intake
87 Wing spar attachment joint
88 Fuselage/rear spar main frame
89 Engine compressor face
90 Forward engine mounting frame

91 Rear fuselage group of fuel tanks
92 Fuel pipe ducting
93 Drop tank tail fins
94 Afterburner duct cooling ram air intake
95 Starboard all-moving tailplane
96 Tailfin construction
97 Fin tip ECM aerials
98 Tail position light
99 Static dischargers
100 Rudder mass balance
101 Rudder
102 Formation light
103 Water injection tank, 30 Imp gal/ (136 l) capacity
104 Rudder power control unit
105 Brake parachute housing
106 Parachute door
107 Petal-type airbrakes, open position
108 Republic convergent/divergent ram air elector nozzle flaps
109 Airbrake/nozzle flap jacks
110 Internal variable area afterburner nozzle
111 Afterburner nozzle actuators
112 Afterburner ducting
113 Tailplane pivot fixing
114 Port all-moving tailplane construction

115 Tailplane titanium box spar
116 Leading edge nose ribs
117 Ventral fuel vent
118 All-moving tailplane control jack
119 Rear fuselage break point
120 Engine firewall
121 Rear engine mounting
122 Engine turbine section heat shroud
123 Engine bay venting ram air intake
124 Rear fuselage frame and stringer construction
125 Runway arrester hook
126 Ventral fin

127 Accessory cooling air duct
128 Cartridge starter
129 Fuselage top longeron
130 Engine driven accessory gearbox
131 Oil tank 3.7 Imp gal (17 l) capacity
132 Pratt & Whitney J75-P-19W turbojet
133 Port Fowler-type flap construction
134 Five section roll control spoilers
135 Flap screw jacks
136 Aileron mass balance

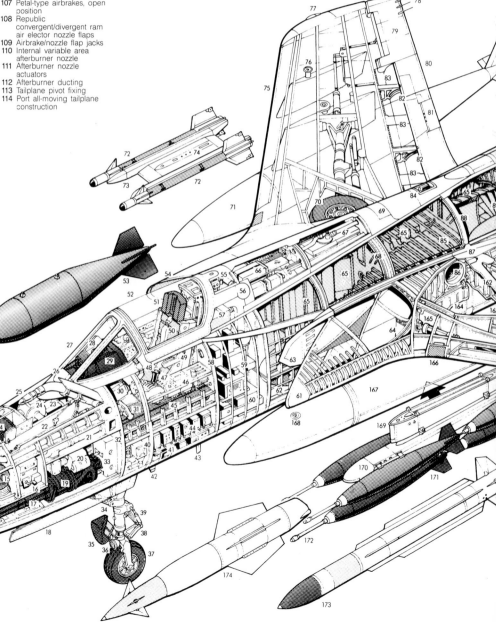

18

Republic F-105 Thunderchief

137 Port drop tank tail fins
138 Honeycomb aileron construction
139 Static dischargers
140 Wing tip fairing
141 Port navigation light
142 AGM-45 Shrike anti-radar missile
143 ECM pod
144 Outboard stores pylon
145 Pylon fixing/fuel filler cap
146 Aileron hinge control

147 Aileron/spoiler mixer linkage
148 Multi-spar wing construction
149 Aileron power control unit
150 Inboard pylon fixing
151 Inboard stores pylon
152 Mainwheel leg door
153 Port mainwheel
154 375 Imp gal (1 705 l) drop tank
155 Main undercarriage leg torque scissor links
156 Landing lamp
157 Port leading edge flap
158 Leading edge flap rotary actuators
159 Main undercarriage pivot mounting
160 Undercarriage side breaker strut
161 Hydraulic retraction jack

AVIAGRAPHICA

162 Diagonal wing spar
163 Mainwheel housing
164 Inner mainwheel door
165 Leading edge flap actuator
166 Leading edge flush aerial
167 541 Imp gal (2 460 l) centreline fuel tank
168 Fuel tank filler cap
169 Centreline stores pylon
170 Triple ejection rack
171 Six M 117 750-lb (340-kg) HE bombs
172 Anti-personnel extended bomb fuse
173 AGM-78 Standard ARM anti-radar missile
174 AGM-12C Bullpup air-to-ground missile

Above: The F-105D-31RE was the last single-seat production version to be built. It was also manufactured in the largest numbers — a total of 135 aircraft.

escalated into a two-year 51 million US Dollars effort carried out in two phases. The first, conducted by the USAF with some assistance from Republic technicians, was completed by November; the second was carried out by Republic, and was completed by mid-1964.

Project Look Alike did much to prepare the aircraft for the demands of sustained operations, and paid off handsomely when the type was sent to war in Vietnam, but in the short term it created new spares shortages. Just as the inadequate stock of spares was being built up, many of the newly-acquired parts were no longer required by the modified aircraft, while growing demands were made for new components introduced by Look Alike.

THE TWO-SEAT F-105F

Since cancellation of the F-105E in 1959, the Thunderchief family had lacked a two-seater which could be used to teach navigation and advanced bombing. Given the complexity of the F-105D, and the magnitude of the task of training new pilots on the type, a two-seater was now urgently required. In May 1962, US Defense Secretary Robert McNamara ordered that a two-seat F-105F version be developed. There would be no increase in planned numbers; the final 143 production F-105Ds were to be built to the new twin-seat standard.

To make room for the second cockpit, the fuselage was stretched by 31in (79cm) and the vertical fin was increased in height. Weight increased by around 2,000lb (907kg). In most other respects, the F-105F was similar to the F-105D, retaining most features of the latter, including the air-refuelling capability.

Progress with the F-105F two-seater was swift, with the first prototype flying ahead of schedule on 11 June 1963 and managing Mach 1.15 on that maiden flight. Category I testing started that summer. The first production example was accepted on 7 December and issued to the 4520th Combat Training Wing at Nellis AFB. The aircraft entered operational service three weeks later on 23 December 1963 with the 4th TFW at Seymour-Johnson AFB.

Commonality between the F-105F and the single-seat F-105D brought advantages and disadvantages. Testing was relatively swift; Category I testing was completed in July 1964, Category II testing a month later. Reliability was as poor as that of the single seater, and the F model would receive the same package of modifications and improvements.

Phase-out of the F-105B from the USAF inventory began in 1964. Both TAC squadrons were eventually re-equipped with the F-105D. The F-105B started its career with the Air National Guard (ANG) in April 1964, but these aircraft were so different to the standard D model as to be of limited use even as trainers. Few saw much ANG service, and by late 1969 the last

Right: With the arrival of the F-105F version in 1963, the USAF finally obtained its long-awaited two-seat Thunderchief. Note the taller tail fin of this version.

SPECIFICATION

F-105D Thunderchief

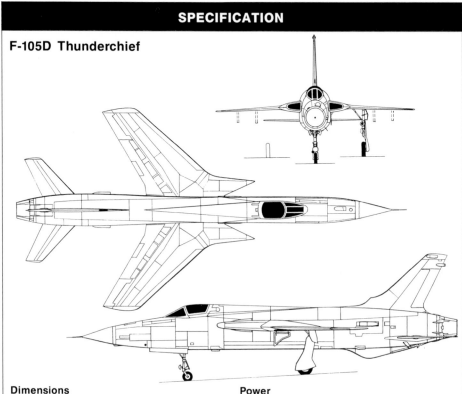

Dimensions
Length: 64ft 5in (19.63m)
Height: 19ft 8in (5.99m)
Wing span: 34ft 11in (10.65m)
Gross wing area: 385ft² (35.78m²)

Weights
Empty: 26,855lb (12,181kg)
Normal take-off weight: 48,976lb (22,215kg)
Maximum take-off weight: 52,838lb (23,967kg)
Maximum external weapons load: 13,000lb (5,900kg)

Power
1 x Pratt & Whitney J75-P-19W turbofan
Maximum thrust: 26,500lb (118kN)
Internal fuel: 1,550 US gal (5,867l)
External fuel: 1,550 US gal (5,867l)

Performance
Maximum speed, high-level: 1,192kts (2,208km/h)
Maximum speed, low-level: 726kts (1,345km/h)
Combat ceiling: 48,500ft (14,780m)
Combat radius: 610nm (1,125km)

examples had been retired.

Early 1964 saw the end of F-105D production. A total of 610 had been built at a unit flyaway cost of 2.14 million US Dollars. This figure was broken down as follows: airframe 1,472,145; engine 244,412; electronics 19,346; armament 167,621; and ordnance 19,346.

At the time, 2.14 million US Dollars seemed a high price to pay for a jet fighter, particularly one which still had a poor reputation for suffering from repeated failures of the engine and fuel system, as well as fuel leaks. The portion of the cost associated with electronics — less than 1 per cent of the total — seems small, even for the relatively simple systems of that era, yet this figure was extracted from an official USAF history. On today's aircraft, the "black boxes" can account for 25 per cent or more of the total unit flyaway cost.

In December 1964, Republic completed the 143rd and final F-105F, bringing production of new-built Thunderchiefs to a close. The final aircraft was delivered to the USAF in January 1964.

Top: When it entered service in 1959, the F-105B made the 335th TFS the first squadron in the world to become operational on Mach 2 strike aircraft.

Below left: This 1969 photo shows the front cockpit of an AGM-78B-equipped EF-105F. The grey-coloured circular screen at top right is for the APR-35 RWR.

Above: With the arrival of the EF-105F, the Wild Weasel squadrons finally had an anti-radar aircraft able to match the escorted formations.

Below: An EF-105F lifts off from Nellis AFB during a November 1967 training mission. Combat-seasoned Weasel crews from Vietnam served as instructors.

THE F-105 was originally developed as a nuclear strike fighter, so the design incorporated a weapon bay in the lower fuselage. Designed to hold a single nuclear weapon, this was 15ft 10in (4.82m) long, 32in (81cm) wide and 32in (81cm) deep. Two hardpoints were provided under each wing, plus two on the centreline. Like the weapons bay, the inboard hardpoints and centreline could also carry what were euphemistically termed ''Special Weapons''. When the Thunderchief was sent to war in South East Asia, its role was that of delivering conventional ordnance, so the weapons bay often used to house a 390USgal fuel tank.

ORDNANCE

Three main types of high-explosive bombs were carried by the Thunderchief: the M-117, Mk 83, and M-118. Widely used by the USAF in the 1960s and 1970s, all had bodies of the modern low-drag profile.

Classified officially as a 750lb bomb, the M-117 weighed 823lb (373kg). Its 89in (226cm) long body had a maximum diameter of 16in (40.6cm), was made from cast steel, and contained 403lb (183kg) of Tritonal or Minol 2 explosive. A typical warload would be six carried on two centreline Multiple Ejection Racks. Various patterns of nose and tail fuzes were used, including an extended nose fuze whose long probe was intended to trigger the

Right: ''Classified'' reads the label on one of the two shrouded weapons beneath the port inlet of this F-105B. Both are late-1950s' vintage tatical nuclear bombs.

weapon before it could bury itself on impact.

The 1,000lb Mk 83 bomb was 118.7in (301.5cm) long and tipped the scales at 985lb (447kg); the cast-steel body held 445lb (202kg) of Tritonal, Minol 2, or H6 explosive. The heaviest of the three was the 3,000lb M-118, with an all-up weight of 3,049lb (1,383kg) and a filling consisting of 1,975lb (895kg) of Tritonal. This

massive weapon was around 185in (470cm) long (the exact length depended on the pattern of fuzes and fins installed), and had a maximum diameter of 24in (61cm).

Other stores cleared for carriage on the F-105D included the M-116A2 and BLU-1B fire bombs. Fabricated from aluminium sheet, the 685lb (311kg) M-116A2 was 137in (348cm) long, 18.6in (47.2cm) in diameter, and

Above: These F-105D-25REs carry "iron" bombs on the centreline, external tanks on the inboard pylons, and launchers for unguided rockets on the outboard pylons.

Below right: Unguided rockets delivered a greater punch than the 0.8in (20mm) gun when used against "soft" targets such as vehicles, troops or radar sites.

Below: An F-150D-6RE with six bombs on the centreline. This was a common loading in Vietnam, as it freed the wing pylons for fuel and self-protection jamming pods.

filled with napalm. The BLU-1/B was similar in size, weighed 697lb (316kg), and contained 90 gallons/615lb (279kg) of napalm. Other free-falling munitions included the MLU-10B 700lb (317kg) mine, and the MC-1 710lb (322kg) chemical bomb.

MISSILES

Strafing ground targets was a role that required massive application of the small amounts of firepower needed to knock out unarmoured targets. Two weapons were widely used for this task: unguided air-to-ground rockets and dispensers for anti-personnel

bomblets. The LAU/3A and LAU/18A each carried 19 unguided rockets, while the LAU-10/A carried four. Systems used for bomblet delivery included the 140lb (63.5kg) SUU-7A/A dispenser, the SUU-30/B dispenser, and the CBU-1/A and -2/A 610lb (276kg) weapons housing 500 and 350 bomblets respectively.

The first guided missile to be carried by the aircraft was the Martin AGM-12 Bullpup. Added by the "Look-Alike" programme, this could be carried on the outboard or inboard underwing hardpoints. By today's standards Bullpup is a primitive weapon, but when the F-105 was designed it represented the latest thing in air-to-ground tactical missiles.

Developed to meet a requirement drawn up in 1953 Bullpup consisted of a standard 250lb (113kg) bomb mounted inside a roll-stabilized canard airframe and powered by an Aerojet-General solid-propellant rocket motor. After launching the weapon, the pilot of the fighter would operate a small cockpit-mounted joystick to keep the missile on the direct line of sight to the target. Guidance commands were sent to the missile via a radio link, where they were used to control four pneumatically-actuated surfaces mounted near the missile nose. Two flares

Armament

located in the tail of the missile helped the pilot track the weapon. This first ASM-N-7 version entered service in 1959, but by 1960 had given way to the improved AGM-12B Bullpup A which used an improved warhead, longer-ranged command link, and a Thiokol LR58 liquid-propellant rocket motor. When production ended in 1970, more than 22,000 rounds had been delivered from US production lines, with a further 8,000 being built in western Europe.

Even in the late 1950s the disadvantages of such "fire and don't forget" guidance were obvious, and Martin started work on an improved version that could be guided from another aircraft, allowing the launch aircraft to break away after weapon release. Originally designated GAM-83A, this led to the definitive AGM-12C (Navy) and -12D (USAF).

A 150lb (68kg) TDU-11/B adaptor allowed AIM-9B Sidewinders to be carried on the outboard hardpoints. This version of Sidewinder was built in large numbers in the late 1950s and early 1960s, many being rebuilt later to the improved AIM-9E and -9J standard. In its original -9B form, the weapon was a simple tail-chase, heat-seeking missile with a maximum range of only 2miles (3.2km). It was rarely used when the F-105 went to war in South East Asia (only two of the 27 MiGs downed by Thunderchiefs were missile kills, while another was despatched by an AIM-9 plus cannon fire).

Above: The Bullpup missile (seen here beneath the wing of an F-105D-10RE) proved disappointing when used in combat. It was manually steered by radio signal.

CANNON

Inevitably for an aircraft of its generation the cannon in question was the General Electric M61 six-barreled 0.8in (20mm) cannon. This rotary cannon has proved irreplaceable, serving on most US fighters to the present day. It armed the highly-agile fighters of the 1970s, and now seems destined to serve well into the next century aboard the new Lockheed F-22 Advanced Tactical Fighter. On the F-105, the M61 is located in a gun bay on the port side of the forward fuselage.

SHRIKE AGM-45

The specialized Wild Weasel two-seat Thunderchiefs, developed during the Vietnam War to locate and destroy enemy radars, were equipped with anti-radiation missiles (ARMs). First to enter service was the AGM-45 Shrike, which was based on the airframe and propulsion system of the AIM-7 Sparrow. It carried a new passive seeker able to home-in onto threat radars, plus a new warhead designed to saturate the target with more than 20,000 steel fragments. Development had started back in 1958, and was spurred by the Cuban procurement of SA-2 Guidelines. Prototypes were tested in 1964, leading to production deliveries to front-line Wild Weasel units in March 1966.

Shrike was to prove a useful weapon. More than 19,000 rounds were built, some of which were updated in the early 1980s. To keep the price down, the US Navy invited a second firm to bid for the task of building production batches, a move which resulted in the unit cost falling from 19,500 to less than 4,000 US Dollars. Even in the early 1990s Shrike remains in the US inventory; it serves on the F-4G and EF-111A and has seen limited export service. Israel was supplied with several hundred configured for anti-Fan Song (SA-2) duties and used them during the 1973 Yom Kippur War. Some still serve on IDFAF Phantoms and Kfirs.

Shrike had tactical limitations. For a start, it must be delivered using a loft manoeuvre that leaves the launch aircraft exposed to hostile defences. If the round is to have a reasonable chance of scoring a kill it must be

Left: 0.8in (20mm) ammunition was carried in a 1,028-round drum in the nose. Also visible is the extended ram-air turbine for emergency hydraulics.

delivered into a "basket", so the launch manoeuvre requires some skill in estimating range and the amount of the gravity drop.

Other problems were the weapon's relatively short range of around five miles (8km), its low speed, and small warhead. The loft manoeuvre at launch was devised to offset gravity drop, but may also help extend the range. In Vietnam, one counter which was used against smart radar operators, who shut down whenever a Weasel came within Shrike range, was to toss-bomb the Shrike round so that the aircraft gave the weapon a range-extending boost.

Early versions shipped to Vietnam had relatively narrow-band seekers, effectively requiring a new version to cope with each new threat. For example, the AGM-45A-3 was designed to counter the Fan Song radar of contemporary SA-2 SAM sites. At least 18 variants were built and, over the years, new electronic technology allowed the seeker of later models to cover a wider bandwidth, thus making them more flexible in combat. By the time that the final AGM-45A-9 and -45A-10 models were built, their seekers covered a greater frequency range than all the previous versions combined.

The weapon also had little off-boresight attack capability. To launch a Shrike successfully, the aircraft had to fly directly towards the target. The missile could not be fired from a turn. If the emitter shut down, the round lost guidance signals and ceased to home.

STANDARD AGM-78

One way of overcoming these tactical limitations was to create a new missile based on a larger and heavier airframe. Again, an off-the-shelf design formed the basis for the new weapon. Standard ARM was based on the RIM-66A Standard naval SAM and

Above: This F-105G Wild Weasel, over Laos in 1972, is armed with AGM-45 Shrike (outboard) and AGM-78 Standard anti-radar missiles (inboard).

weighed more than 1,350lb (612kg). Addition of the custom-designed LAU-78 and -80 pylons needed to mate this SAM derivative to a tactical aircraft took the all-up weight of a single AGM-78 installation to almost 1,600lb (725kg), a figure that does not include the specialized avionics that must be installed within the launch aircraft to handle the task of sorting and identifying the enemy radar signals.

A classic example of a US "crash" programme, it was rushed into service to supplement the shorter-ranged Shrike. Studies began in 1966, with development being ordered late that year. First flight of a Standard ARM was in the summer of 1967, and by March of the following year the weapon had been deployed to South East Asia.

A modification scheme to enable 14 Wild Weasel F-105Fs to carry Standard Mod Zero was completed in February 1968, but the first combat firing was made by a US Navy A-6B Intruder on 6 March. First combat launch from an EF-105F did not take place until 10 May that year.

Standard was a great improvement over Shrike. Its range was greater (more than 25km), and it could be fired at off-boresight targets. A Wild Weasel crew no longer needed to fly a predictable course directly towards their target, but could launch a Standard round and leave this to make the turn on to the target bearing.

AGM-78 was able to operate against several frequency bands, but had to be manually programmed before flight. It could also "remember" the location of the target, continuing its attack even if the target radar shut down.

From nose to tail, a Standard ARM was made up of a guidance section (housing the seeker, signal processing electronics, and guidance computer); ordnance section (incorporating a warhead fitted with impact and proximity fuzes); autopilot/battery section, dual-thrust rocket motor; spacer section (used to house smoke generators); and the steering control section which contained all of the control surface actuators.

First version into service was the AGM-78A Mod O. Designed for use against the SA-2 Guideline, this used the seeker-head from the AGM-45A-3 version of Shrike. The A-2 model introduced a red phosphorous smoke marker. Carried in the spacer section, this provided aircraft equipped with conventional ordnance with clear indication of the target position and allowed them to move in to complete the destruction of a radar or SAM site struck by a Standard ARM. The A-4 model had an improved seeker able to cope with some types of Soviet early-warning and GCI radar.

IN early October 1962 the US government found itself faced with evidence that the Soviet Union was installing long-range nuclear missiles on the island of Cuba. On 18 October, the 4th Tactical Fighter Wing (of which the 334th and 335th TFS formed part) was alerted for war. Three days later it was ordered to redeploy to McCoy AFB, Florida. Short of aircraft due to Project Look Alike, the 4th TFW had to borrow some Thunderchiefs from the 4520th Combat Crew Training Wing at Nellis AFB, Nevada.

At 04:00hrs on 22 October, the unit was placed on one-hour alert, with pilots and bombed-up aircraft waiting for the go order. At 10:00hrs, President Kennedy announced a naval blockade of Cuba and, that afternoon, alert time was cut to 15min.

The order to fly came on 27 October, the day a Cuban SAM site shot down a USAF U-2 flying along the northern coast of the island. Instead of the anticipated strike against the Cuban missile sites, the 4th TFW pilots found themselves flying air-superiority missions, patrolling the skies of southern Florida to guard against possible last-minute air raids by Cuban Ilyushin Il-28 Beagle light bombers.

The crisis ended on the following day when Premier Khrushchev announced that the missiles would be removed and returned to the Soviet Union. The 4th TFW and its Thunderchiefs returned to Seymour

Right and far right: The F-105's ability to take combat damage and keep flying became legendary as the type played a major role in the bombing of North Vietnam.

Johnson AFB on 29 November. Combat debut for the Thunderchief would not take place for another two years, and would happen on the other side of the world.

DEBUT IN SOUTH EAST ASIA

On 2 August 1964, the US Navy destroyer USS *Maddox*, then on patrol in the Gulf of Tonkin, reported that she had come under attack from North Vietnamese torpedo boats. Two days later, the 4th TFW received an F-105D which looked very different to those which equipped its four Thunderchief squadrons. The new-

Above: Aircraft 64-4435 was the first EF-105F to be rebuilt to the full F-105G specification, complete with QRC-380 (ALQ-105) blisters fixed on the fuselage sides.

comer was the first to carry a camouflage finish. On the following day, one of its squadrons — the 334th — left Florida to begin the long flight to Thailand. Other F-105Ds from the 18th TFW left Okinawa, also bound for Thailand, as part of a military build-up which included F-100 and F-102 fighters.

During an August sortie over the Plaine des Jarres in Laos, four F-105D

of 36th Squadron (part of the 18th TFW which had moved to Thailand from Okinawa) were fired on by a communist anti-aircraft battery. One was hit and badly damaged, but the pilot was able to fly it back to base at Korat, Thailand. It was the first demonstration of the Republic aircraft's ability to take combat damage and keep flying.

Four days after arriving in Thailand, the 334th flew its first combat mission. During the next five months of its tour of duty, this squadron would fly an average of 15 sorties per day, an impressive record for an aircraft which at that time had an unenviable reputation for unreliability

November saw the arrival of another 4th TFW Thunderchief unit, the 335th TFS. By the following March, the 334th and 335th had returned to the USA and were being used to train F-105D pilots for combat. In October, all four squadrons of the 4th TFW had traded in their "Thuds" and were converting to the F-4D Phantom.

By early 1965, additional F-105Ds were becoming available as this aircraft was retired from the USAFE. As the 36th and 49th TFWs converted to F-4 Phantoms, their F-105s were flown back to the USA and issued to the 23rd TFW at McConnell AFB, Kansas, the training unit for pilots being sent to Vietnam.

Above: July 1964 — an F-105D-31RE enjoys the last months of peace. In August, 334th TFS would fly to Thailand in order to begin combat operations in SE Asia.

but was ordered instead to conduct a lower-intensity campaign aimed at reducing the infiltration of men and equipment from the north.

It would be an unhappy experience for the USAF, USN and USMC aircrew who had been sent to war. Political constraints imposed by Washington made missions largely ineffective. For example, on 2 March, the opening day of Rolling Thunder, only 25 of the force of around 150 F-105Ds in the region were ordered into action as part of the combined US and South Vietnamese air strikes.

When the war had started in August of the previous year, the North Vietnamese air defences had been based on around 1,400 anti-aircraft guns plus a network of 22 early-warning radars and only four fire-control radars. By the outbreak of Rolling Thunder, nine more early-warning radars had been added, plus five more fire-control radars, and a mixed fleet of around 30 MiG-15 and MiG-17 subsonic fighters.

Important targets during early

ROLLING THUNDER

That spring, President Johnson ordered Rolling Thunder, a bombing campaign against North Vietnam. The USAF had wanted permission to conduct a 16-day intensive campaign against 94 targets in North Vietnam,

Right: This Thailand-based F-105D-10RE of the 44th TFS carries standard bombs on the centreline, but those on the outer wing pylons have extended fuzes.

Combat

Rolling Thunder strikes included road and rail bridges and radar sites between the demilitarized zone (DMZ), on the 17th parallel and the 19th parallel some 150miles (240km) south of Hanoi. If these transportation links could be cut, planners argued, then the flow of men and supplies to the south would dwindle.

THE THANH HOA BRIDGE

On 3 April US fighters attempted to destroy the recently-built Thanh Hoa combined road/rail bridge over the Song Ma River. A force of 79 aircraft, including 46 Thunderchiefs, was despatched to attack the 504ft (164.5m) long bridge, and its nearby anti-aircraft gun defences, with bombs and Bullpup missiles. North Vietnamese Air Force (NVAF) MiG-17s intercepted the strike, but the attackers pressed home their attack. Despite repeated hits, however, the bridge survived.

On 4 April, the attackers were back for another try and so were the MiGs. One Thunderchief was shot down by a 1.5in (37mm) anti-aircraft gun, two more by a flight of four NVAF MiG-17 fighters. The bridge was badly damaged, but neither of its two spans were downed. Next attack was on 7 May, when 28 aircraft scored multiple hits with 750lb (340kg) bombs. On 30 May, the "Thuds" were back for what would prove their final attempt to down the bridge. A four-aircraft flight hit the bridge, closing it for repairs but failing to inflict permanent damage.

It was an unsuccessful start to a long and difficult campaign of attempts at bridge-busting. Experience soon showed that the massive concrete structure of a large bridge was very difficult to damage by air strikes. Not until the arrival of the first laser-guided bombs (LGBs) in the final stages of the war would such structures become really vulnerable.

IMPROVING THE "THUD"

Over the next three years, the Thunderchief became the major strike aircraft used against North Vietnam. While the B-52 strategic bomber was regularly used to strike against tactical targets in South Vietnam, the Thunderchief — designed as a tactical fighter — flew most of the strategic bombing missions against the North. It was a "meatgrinder" which imposed massive attrition on the fleet, forcing the USAF to strip its USAFE and TAC Thunderchief units of aircraft in order to maintain the strength of the strike force in South East Asia.

Turning what had until then been a disappointing aircraft into the premier strike fighter of the Vietnam War required extensive modifications. These improved reliability, safety and survivability; they also re-equipped an aircraft designed for the nuclear strike mission to allow it to deliver heavy loads of conventional ordnance.

Armour plating was installed, to make the aircraft less vulnerable to ground fire, along with backup flight controls. Avionics changes included fitting an ASG-19 sighting systems, plus an X-band radar beacon. The ejection seat was improved and changes were made to the troublesome flight refuelling probe fitted to early F-105Ds.

Republic had planned to fit the internal fuel tanks with a fire detection and suppression system, but this had been deleted by the USAF to save weight and cost. It now had to be retrofitted as a costly modification.

Despite its good handling qualities once airborne, the Thunderchief did have problems due to its high wing loading and low thrust:weight ratio.

Right: In-flight refuelling allowed the F-105D to range deep into North Vietnamese skies. Connected to the boom of a tanker, this aircraft is venting its fuel.

Even in USAFE service it had acquired the reputation of being runway-hungry, with an 8,000ft (2,438m) strip being a bit tight for regular operations; 10,000ft (3,048m) was preferable. In the warm climate of Thailand, pilots would need every last bit of thrust increase available from the F-105 water-injection system. Bomb loads often had to be limited to improve take-off performance, and to make sure that the loaded Thunderchiefs would be able to climb to the operating altitude of the tanker aircraft on which they relied.

SUPPLY INTERDICTION

Interdicting the flow of supplies from China to Vietnam was another major goal of the US bombing campaign, so regular attacks were mounted on the

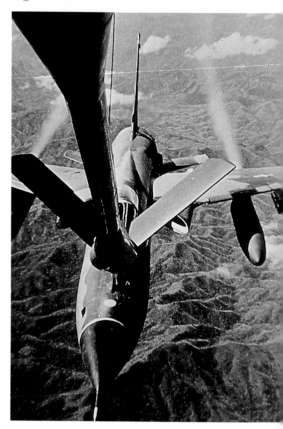

Left: Taking off from Korat, Thailand, in August 1968, this heavily-loaded F-105D needed all the power it could get from afterburning and water injection.

THE SAM THREAT

US reconnaissance aircraft detected the construction of the first Soviet SA-2 Guideline SAM site 15miles (24km) south-east of Hanoi on 5 April 1965. As its designation suggests, the SA-2 was one of the first Soviet SAM systems. The earlier SA-1 Guild has been deployed only around Moscow, but the SA-2 had become the Soviet's main long-range SAM system.

Each SA-2 missile was around 35ft (10.7m) long, 20in (50cm) in diameter, and weighing about 5,000lb (2,268kg). Thrust into the air by a solid-propellent booster, the missile combined liquid-propellent cruise propulsion with radar command guidance. In 1960 the SA-2 had downed the CIA's high-flying Lockheed U-2 spy plane over Soviet territory, then again in 1962 shot another down over Cuba during the Cuban Missile Crisis. Having proved its effectiveness against the

Left: Taking off from Korat, Thailand, in August 1968, this heavily-loaded F-105D needed all the power it could get from afterburning and water injection.

two railway lines which connected the two nations. One ran north-west from Hanoi, following the Red River into China where it headed toward Kunming; the other ran north-east from Hanoi to connect the capital with Nanning. Between the two lay a mountain ridge. A familiar sight to pilots tasked with attacking the railroads, it was to become known as ''Thud Ridge'' — a location where many battle-damaged F-105s would crash in the years to come.

One problem with the north-eastern railway line was that much of its length lay in ''sanctuary'' areas — parts of North Vietnam which the US government had declared off limits to the US strike aircraft. Air strikes were not permitted within 10nm (16km) of central Hanoi or 4nm (6.4km) from the centre of the port of Haiphong. Severe restrictions were placed on air operations within 30nm (48km) of Hanoi and 10nm (16km) of Haiphong, and a buffer zone between 26 and 30nm (42-48km) deep was declared along the border with the People's

Republic of China. MiG bases were also not to be attacked.

Only 10miles of line therefore ran through territory in which air strikes were permitted. Not surprisingly, the North Vietnamese crammed a staggering 1,100 anti-aircraft guns along that stretch of track. Bridges were still regarded as key targets and in mid-May US aircraft attacked bridges on the rail links to China. By this time a new threat to US aircraft had emerged with Soviet-supplied SA-2 surface-to-air missiles (SAMs).

Below: An F-105D flies formation with a US Navy F-4C. Attempts to get the Thunderchief returned to production were in vain; the USAF adapted the F-4C instead.

Combat

U-2, the system threatened US control of the skies over North Vietnam. Thunderchief pilots must have regretted the misguided decision back in 1959 to strip the F-105D of EW systems in order to save money. It is unlikely that any of those responsible for that decision ever had to fly over "Thud Ridge".

By June the first sites were operational, and a total of six had been detected by mid-July. None were used operationally until 24 July when a site west of Hanoi fired three rounds at a formation of four F-4C Phantoms flying around 55miles (88km) northwest of Hanoi; one aircraft was downed and the others damaged. Three days later a force of 46 F-105 Thunderchiefs pounded the missile site into silence.

SAM deployments continued. Despite the size and weight of its components, the SA-2 system was readily transportable, so could be moved swiftly to protect tactical targets under threat (such as bridges and rail junctions). During August, 11 more SAMs were fired at US aircraft which resulted in two kills.

One way of avoiding SAMs was to fly fast and low. At such levels the SAMs were impotent, but the aircraft could be fired on by anti-aircraft guns of every calibre. A compromise altitude of around 4,500ft (1,372m) blunted the effectiveness of the SAMs while being above the effective envelope of the smaller-calibre, anti-aircraft guns.

On 5 October 24 F-105Ds of the 562nd TFS formed part of a massive operation aimed at knocking out the Lang Met rail bridge 50miles (80km) north-west of Hanoi. Each carried two 3,000lb (1,361kg) bombs plus a 650gal centreline tank. Flak in the target area was intense and was supplemented by SAMs. Despite this, good hits were scored on the centre span. The bridge went down, but only eight of the

562nd TFs's Thunderchiefs made it back to their base at Takhli. Three of the others had been shot down and the remainder had taken enough battle damage to require diversion to airfields in South Vietnam.

THE ANTI-RADAR ROLE

A week after the destruction of the first SA-2 site, a meeting was held to discuss possible countermeasures to the Soviet missile. For the moment, the only available solution was to locate sites by traditional reconnaissance then attack them using standard fighter-bombers. By the end of the year, the US forces would have destroyed seven more SAM sites by means of set-piece raids, but lost eight aircraft in doing so: three Thunderchiefs, plus two F-8 Crusaders, two F-4 Phantoms, and a single A-4 Skyhawk. Total Thunderchief combat losses for the year totalled 60 — almost eight per cent of the entire F-105D/F fleet.

The weakness of the SA-2 system was identified as its dependence on a shelter-mounted Fan Song radar used to track both the target aircraft and the missile in flight; several programmes were launched to exploit this.

By late 1965 the F-105D, like many US tactical fighters deployed to South East Asia, was being retrofitted with the APR-25 and -26 radar warning

receivers. Developed by Applied Technology Inc (ATI), and originally known as Vector IV and WR-300 respectively, the units had different functions. The APR-25 operated in S, C and X-band, and was intended to warn aircrew if their aircraft was being illuminated by a hostile radar. The APR-26 monitored the frequencies used by the SA-2 command link and would warn if a SAM had been launched. Other efforts such as QRC-160 developed add-on jamming pods which could be carried to counter North Vietnamese radars. Throughout the war, a series of gradually-improving systems such as the ALQ-71, -72 -87 and -101 would be fielded to deal with the latest ground-based and fighter radars used by the North Vietnamese.

Destruction of its radars would effectively blind an SA-2 battery, but the USAF and USN lacked the specialized weapons needed to locate and destroy hostile radars, particularly aircraft able to detect and home in on hostile emitters.

Tests of F-100 Super Sabres fitted with experimental QRC-253-2 radar-

Right: This F-105G of the 561st TFS wears its peeling paint like a battle honour. Delays with the Wild Weasel F-4 forced the -105G to serve until the end of the war.

Left: During an air strike in late October 1965 against a railroad bridge about 110 miles (180km) north-east of Hanoi, an F-105D fires its AGM-12 Bullpup missile.

homing receivers had been carried out in 1964. The results in flights against US Hawk missile sites had been good enough to cause Bendix to propose in the following spring that specialized anti-radar aircraft be creating by equipping some F-100s with a radar-homing & warning receiver (RHAWR). In retrospect, it seems incredible that the USAF rejected the idea at a time when the US was embarking on a war in South East Asia.

In great secrecy, a crash programme was launched to develop an anti-radar version of the F-100. Code-named Wild Weasel 1, it saw seven, two-seat F-100Fs modified to receive the APR-25 and -26 radar-warning receivers, plus the 2-4GHz IR-133 panoramic receiver, a more sensitive system able to detect SA-2 signals at longer range than the APR-25. Designated ''Wild Weasels'', these were flown by pilots from TAC and EW operators from SAC. Some of these ex-B-52 EW officers found the manoeuvrability of a fighter hard to cope with; in the words of a contemporary song: ''Pilots quaking, EWOs barfing, off we go to war''.

Some EW officers were horrified to learn that they'd be assigned to the back seat of a jet fighter which would deliberately go looking for SAMs. The reaction of one — ''You've got to be ****** me!'' — became the unofficial motto of the first Weasel unit.

A detachment of four aircraft was rushed to the 388th TFW at Korat in Thailand in November 1965. The aircraft arrived on 25 November and combat missions started on 1 December, less than four months after the meeting which had launched the

programme and just 90 days after completion of the first aircraft.

These early flights, code-named Iron Hand, saw the two-seat Wild Weasels leading flights of F-105 Thunderchiefs. One of the six F-100F was lost to AA fire on 20 December, but the remaining crews continued to hone their skills, learning the art of terrain masking (using high ground to screen the aircraft from enemy radars crews). On 22 December an F-100F escorted by five F-105s destroyed a SAM site near the Red River.

Above: Armed with underwing Shrike missiles, and with the sunlight catching its ALQ-105 blister, this 388th TFW F-105G waits on the flightline at Korat.

Below: Hunter and killer — this Bullpup-armed F-105D-31RE of the 333rd TFS will attack targets detected, then pinpointed by the escorting 354th TFS EF-105F.

Combat

The F-100F installation proved the Wild Weasel concept, and the nickname "Bear" for a Wild Weasel backseater was also coined around this time. The remaining three aircraft were deployed in late February 1966, arriving in time to act as replacements for one F-100F lost in an accident and another shot down by ground fire.

No more F-100F Wild Weasels were built; the F-100 lacked the performance of the Thunderchiefs it was trying to protect, forcing the latter to slow down so that their Weasel escorts could keep up. The only long-term solution would be a Wild Weasel based on a Mach 2 fighter.

The only major improvement introduced during the F-100F Wild Weasel's brief combat career was the installation of the Texas Instruments AGM-45 Shrike anti-radiation missile (ARM) in March 1966. Taken into action for the first time on 18 April, Shrike was initially used in the less defended areas of North Vietnam until operation tactics had been proven; but by the summer of 1966 aircraft were ranging deep into hostile airspace, attacking SAM sites and destroying the specialized radars such as Fan Song which were used for missile tracking and guidance.

WILD WEASEL EF-105s

Even before the F-100Fs had reached South East Asia, work was under way to create higher-performance anti-radar aircraft. The first attempt to develop an anti-radar version of the Thunderchief was code-named Wild Weasel 1A. Tested soon after the F-100F in the autumn of 1965, this involved two F-105Ds fitted with a RHAWR installation plus the AZ/EL sight. The latter projected steering cues onto the combining glass of the gunsight, creating what was effectively a primitive head-up display. It worked, but the pilot workload was judged

Above: A Shrike-armed EF-105F releases bombs from its centreline pylon. Wild Weasels normally operated at low altitude; this sort of high-altitude attack was rare.

too high. The two-seat F-105F would be needed for any operational anti-radar Thunderchief.

This first took shape in the form of Wild Weasel 2. Near-contemporary with Wild Weasel IA, this was an F-105F fitted with a Bendix-developed RHAWR. Although the system was later deployed on other aircraft as the APS-107, it was rejected in favour of the avionics fitted in the Super Sabre Weasels.

The F-105F had the range and payload-carrying capacity for deep strikes into hostile territory, but being out of production it was available in slowly dwindling numbers. The best solution, the DoD decided, would be to base long-term plans on a Weasel version of the F-4 Phantom. Two projects were launched: Wild Weasel 3 would fit a batch of F-105Fs with similar avionics to those of the F-100F; while Wild Weasel 4 would perform similar surgery on the F-4 Phantom, giving the USAF a more manoeuvrable Weasel with a better chance in air-to-air combat if jumped by MiGs and one which, because it

was based on a production aircraft, could be ordered in quantity as required.

Conversion of Thunderchiefs for the new role went smoothly and took about eight days per aircraft. The main systems added were the APR-25 radar-warning receiver, APR-26 launch-warning receiver, and IR-300C panoramic receiver, plus the AZ/EL sighting system tested on the Wild Weasel IA F-105Ds. While this was going on, F-100F Wild Weasel crews from South East Asia acted as instructors on a six-week course intended to train pilots and EW operators for the new aircraft.

On 15 January 1966, the first prototype of what became unofficially known as the EF-105F had been test-flown for the first time. The hurriedly installed systems gave problems and the first six EF-105Fs had to be further modified. By mid-March solutions had been found and five aircraft were prepared for the journey to South East Asia.

By this time seven Thunderchief squadrons were already there, flying

Right: F-105D pilot Major Ralph Robertson watches as other Thunderchiefs in the same formation take on fuel before heading into North Vietnam.

a total of around 140 aircraft from two bases in Thailand: Korat and Takhli. As the USAF groomed the newly-arrived EF-105s for action, the North Vietnamese were also starting to operate a new warplane in the MiG-21 Fishbed.

The EF-105s arrived in Thailand on 28 May, three days before the Thunderchief fleet took part in one of the largest raids mounted to date. Air strikes against a storage complex at Yen Bay damaged or destroyed 118 warehouses used to store military supplies and equipment. The first EF-105F Wild Weasel mission took place on 3 June, with the new aircraft flying under the lead of one of the surviving F-100Fs.

The first mission led by an EF-105F (the scheduled F-100F lead aircraft had aborted the mission) occured on 6 June, while the next day saw the first "kill" of a North Vietnamese radar, a GCI set knocked out by a volley of unguided rockets. Night missions started on 17 June.

A modification programme added a new sensor to the EF-105F. Known as SEE-SAMS(B), this was another launch-warning receiver better able to monitor SA-2 launch activity. It was first used operationally on 1 July, and two days later SEE-SAM(B)-equipped EF-105Fs knocked out an SA-2 site

near Hanoi. The Thunderchiefs rapidly took over the anti-radar mission from the surviving F-100Fs; the final Wild Weasel sortie of the latter aircraft was on 11 July. Many of these early kills were achieved using unguided rockets or even cannon fire, but the AGM-45 Shrike soon became a major part of the EF-105F armament.

MIG DEFENDERS

Another opponent faced by the F-105 units were NVAF MiG fighters. Although these small and agile fighters had limited success in air-to-air combat — some two-thirds of all US warplanes lost over the North were shot down by anti-aircraft gunfire — their habit of "jumping" bomb-ladened strike aircraft sometimes forced the latter to jettison their ordnance and light the afterburner to escape.

Hunting MiGs was not part of the Thunderchief's job, but pilots who found themselves able to deliver a burst of 0.8in (20mm) cannon fire into a Soviet-built fighter were happy to do so. On 29 June 1966 Maj. Fred

Above: By January 1968 when this photo was taken at Da Nang, South Vietnam, around half the "Thud" force had been lost and the F-4 was playing an ever-growing role.

Tracy of the 388th TFW became the first F-105 pilot to down a MiG. When four MiGs attacked a flight of Thunderchiefs engaged on an Iron Hand defence-suppression mission north-west of Hanoi, one managed to score several hits on Tracy's aircraft; as it overshot the damaged F-105, Tracy fired at it. The MiG-17 rolled over and flew a split S manoeuvre down into the cloud. Tracy was unable to follow due to the damage his aircraft had sustained and the low-altitude of the cloud layer — only 2,000ft (609m) above ground level. He was credited with a "kill". Two other Thunderchiefs in the same formation also fired at MiGs.

Kills nevertheless built up rapidly as the EF-105F crews gained experience. On 4 July, a single flight knocked out four radars. Luck was bound to run out, however, and by late August 1966,

Combat

five of the first 11 EF-105F had been lost in action. The small force was boosted by the arrival of 10 more converted aircraft.

A new and more intensive phase of air-to-air combat began on 4 September. On all but four days, North Vietnamese MiGs attempted to engage US air strikes. Three of the five MiG-17s shot down by F-105Ds in 1966 were downed during this period.

IMPROVING PROTECTION

1966 saw the start of two long-running upgrade schemes for the Thunderchief. The first allowed the aircraft to carry wing-mounted EW pods. The other was aimed at modifying a batch of 30 F-105Ds to give an improved nav/attack system, able to provide better navigational data, and the ability to deliver more accurate visual and blind-bombing attacks. The central component of the latter scheme was the new ARN-85 LORAN system. Before long, it became obvious that the ARN-85 had two fundamental problems: poor reliability and rising cost. A better alternative would have to be found, and that would take time. Wild Weasel operations remained

difficult, given that in the autumn of 1966 North Vietnam had deployed more than 100 SAM sites, a figure which would rise to between 150 and 170 by early 1967. Better training would obviously help, so the former F-100F crews were used as instructors at the 4537th Fighter Weapons School at Nellis AFB. What had been a four-week training course was expanded, first to six weeks and then to 12.

By the end of 1966, US aircrews had flown more than 1,000 sorties against bridge targets that year. The F-105 had played a major part in that year's campaign and had paid the price. A loss rate which had peaked at eight in two days had seen a total of 111 lost in action. Worried planners added that total to the 60 lost the previous year and began to wonder how far the Thunderchief fleet was from extinction. For F-105 pilots, the chances of surviving a tour of 100 missions seemed slim.

One way of tipping the balance in the ''Thud's'' favour was to maul the North Vietnamese fighter force. On 2 January 1967 a formation of F-4Cs flew slowly into North Vietnamese airspace, hoping to look like a formation of bomb-ladened F-105s when

viewed by Vietnamese radar. The trick worked and seven MiGs were shot down when the Phantoms accelerated to battle speed and turned the tables on the Soviet-built fighters. The chastening experience would keep the North Vietnamese Air Force docile until March.

St. Valentine's Day saw the start of a more intensive bombing campaign directed at important targets including railways, repair facilities and power stations. Many had previously been left unattacked thanks to their being in sanctuary areas such as those around Hanoi and Haiphong, and in the buffer zone along the Chinese border. From 23 April onwards, target lists were expanded to include North Vietnamese military airfields.

Since the war began, crews had been arguing for permission to attack North Vietnamese airfields, but this had always been refused by Washington. Kep, to the north-east of Hanoi, and Hoa Lac, to the west, were early targets, but strikes were soon mounted against all bases able to operate jet fighters. The MiG-21s were eventually pulled back to bases in China, from where they were once more able to fly combat missions against USAF forces.

With the growing availability of self-protection EW pods, Wild Weasel EF-105s, and F-4 Phantoms for fighter escort, things became a little easier for the strike formations. Other less-publicized F-105F variants were also deployed to blunt the effectiveness of the North Vietnamese radar defences. Under the Combat Martin programme, several F-105Fs were fitted with QRC-128 VHF jammers, and used to interfere with communications

Above: F-105Ds of the 34th TFS salvo 750lb (340kg) bombs onto a target in North Vietnam. At this altitude, US aircraft were a prime target for SA-2 Guideline missiles.

between North Vietnamese MiGs and the GCI (Ground Controlled Interception) control centres on which they relied for tactical instructions and information. Another project code-named Commando Nail fitted some F-105Fs with modified R-14A radars whose expanded displays gave a more detailed image of ground targets, plus facilities which allowed the back-seater to initiate weapon release. These Command Nail Thunderchiefs were used for low-level night missions, bombing by radar; their first sortie was on 26 April 1967.

THE AIR WAR INTENSIFIES

The spring raids goaded the MiGs into flying repeated intercept missions, and the Thunderchief pilots did their bit to hit back at the fighters sent against them. During a strike mission against the Thai Nguyen steelworks north of Hanoi, Capt. Max Brestel shot down two MiG-17s, the first to fall

to the F-105s in that year. Another would go down on 26 March, while April saw seven more credited to F-105s, plus six more in June. Even the Wild Weasels got into the air-to-air combat scene, with Maj. Leo Thorsness scoring the first EF-105F MiG kill on 19 April. He fired at another, which was last seen spiralling downwards but he was not credited with a kill in this case. By early June this level of combat attrition had forced the MiGs to avoid combat once more, a lull which would last through June and July.

When Thailand-based F-105s and F-4s attacked the Paul Doumer rail bridge on 11 August, the MiGs rose to challenge them. Built by the French in 1902, the 5,532ft (1,686m) bridge had 19 spans and was the longest in Vietnam. It lay across the Red River on the outskirts of Hanoi and handled an average of 26 trains per day.

Given their experience with other bridges, those planning the strike knew how hard it was to damage concrete and steel. Little more than four hours before take-off, orders had been sent to swap the standard 750lb (340kg) bombs already fitted to the Thunderchiefs for 3,000lb (1,361kg) bombs. The strike force which attacked the bridge consisted of six flights, three of F-105 strike aircraft, one of EF-105F Wild Weasels, another for the flak suppression, and the last as MIGCAP. The chosen tactic was a 45deg dive attack after a pull up to 13,000ft (3,960m). Down went some 94tons of bombs and down went three spans of the bridge. The rail route would remain closed until early October.

Below: The F-105G Wild Weasel would become the definitive anti-radar strike aircraft, serving through the war, then in Europe, and, finally, with US-based units.

Combat

STEMMING THE LOSS RATE

By mid-1967, several potential "Thud" problems were emerging to join the long-running technical troubles to which the aircraft was prone. Combat attrition was now a major problem; as was the fact that most F-105s had clocked up 1,500 flying hours, while some were past the 2,000-hour mark. Heavy use of afterburner in combat was creating problems with the engine, while shortage of spares forced regular cannibalization of some aircraft to keep the others flying.

That summer, Republic's engineers devised a modification which would greatly reduce the aircraft's vulnerability to combat damage. Although the Thunderchief was fitted with main and back-up hydraulic systems, in the aft fuselage just ahead of the tailplane, these were routed in close proximity to one another. Combat damage in this area which knocked out one system often took out the other at the same time. As the hydraulics failed, the all-moving tailplane would rise and then lock itself in that position, forcing the aircraft into a dive.

It was obviously impractical in wartime to perform the sort of airframe surgery needed to provide greater mechanical separation between the two systems, so Republic devised instead a modification which would allow the pilot to lock the tail surfaces if he realized that both hydraulic systems were failing. If this was done while the tail surfaces were still in the horizontal position, the aircraft might be able to keep flying for long enough to get the pilot away from the immediate

Right: Ejector racks empty, an F-105D approaches a KC-135 to refuel for the return trip to base in 1968. Note the jamming pod on the port outboard pylon.

combat zone, or even out to sea or over friendly territory. Roll control could be obtained by use of differential flap (another modification introduced around this time). These facilities wouldn't save the damaged "Thud", but did greatly improve the pilot's chances of a safe ejection and successful rescue by friendly forces.

Other changes added a third hydraulic system; duplicate fuel system; installed fire-suppressing foam inside the fuel tanks and into surrounding cavities; and fitted a fire-extinguishing system. Another survival aid was a new zero-zero ejection seat.

By August, the loss rate was declining thanks to a combination of better training and tactics, Wild Weasel and MIGCAP support, and the measure of protection provided by EW systems such as the ALQ-17, ALQ-72 and ALQ-87 jamming pods.

Thunderchiefs revisited the Paul Doumer bridge on 25 October. Such repeat raids were common, given the skill of the North Vietnamese in repairing bomb damage. Once again, 3,000lb (1,361kg) bombs were used to knock out two spans and a supporting pier. By 20 November, it would be in use once more and back on the US target list.

Another raid that day saw Thunderchiefs strike at Phuc Yen airfield. Close to Hanoi, and thus off limits to US attack until now, it was the largest air base in North Vietnam. The runway was cratered and four MiGs destroyed on the ground with a further eight damaged. Once again, repair crews soon fixed the damage to the runway and Phuc Yen was operational in a week or so.

Bad weather prevented a further attack on the Paul Doumer bridge

in South East Asia, it was obvious that the aircraft's service days were numbered and unlikely to stretch beyond 1970.

The Thunderchief was well-liked by its crews. By the end of the year, more than 250 of them had clocked up the 100 missions needed in order to return to the USA. The only thing wrong with the "Thud", pilots argued, was that there weren't enough of them. Proposals had been drawn up in mid-1967 to re-open the Thunderchief production line and build a further 300 aircraft, but the scheme was eventually rejected the following summer. As the 1960s drew to a close, the F-4 Phantom would take over from the F-105 as the main workhorse of the air war against North Vietnam.

A NEW THUD: THE F-105G

Early 1968 was a bad time for the US forces in Vietnam. The Tet Offensive demonstrated the uncanny ability of the Viet Cong to strike within the cities of South Vietnam, while the siege of the Marine garrison at Khe Sahn threatened to become another Dien Bien Phu. The siege of Khe Sahn would last until April, and breaking it required US aircraft — everything from tactical fighters to B-52 strategic bombers — to deliver

until mid-December. Two attacks were needed in mid-December for the 3,000lb (1,361kg) bombs to inflict lasting damage. This time, the bridge would be knocked out of action for several months.

By the end of 1967, 87 Thunderchiefs had been lost in action that year. In air-to-air combat, F-105Ds had shot down 20 MiG-17s, with F-105Fs claiming a further three. Only three of 28 MiG-17s downed by Thunderchiefs during the Vietnam War were hit by Sidewinder missiles; most were gun "kills", and even one of the few Sidewinder victims had also been attacked using the cannon.

At around 1.6 aircraft lost/1,000 sorties flown, the F-105 loss rate was half that experienced in 1965 and well below the 2.7/1,000 of 1966. Even so, around 318 "Thuds" had now been lost in combat, a further 39 in accidents. This amounted to almost half of the 610 D and 143 F models which had been built. With between 130 and 140 deployed in total by the two wings

Above: F-105G Wild Weasels from the 561st TFS (tailcode WW) and 17th TFS (JB) await their turn to refuel from a KC-135 tanker en route back to Korat.

Below: Shrike-armed 561st TFS Wild Weasels formate with a KC-135. Hanoi is some 450 miles (725km) from Korat, a long haul for the "Thud's" J75 turbojet.

Combat

35,000 tons of ordnance on the enemy positions around the beleaguered base.

While the ground forces fought back within the cities, the F-105s carried the war back north in the latest phase of Rolling Thunder. Targets included bridges, railyards, power stations and airfields. Phuc Yen was raided again on 14 January.

By early 1968 the two EF-105F squqadrons in South East Asia, the 13th and 354th TFS, were credited with the destruction of 89 SAM sites and three MiG-17s. A high price was still being paid in men and machines with 26 EF-105Fs lost in action, along with 42 aircrew captured, killed or missing in action. The chances of a Weasel crew completing a tour of 100 missions seemed minimal. Maj. Leo Thorsness, the first Weasel pilot to down a MiG, was shot down on his 92nd mission; he and his "Bear" were to survive six years of captivity.

A series of modifications helped keep the EF-105F combat effective, with the aircraft gradually receiving improved RHAW and launch-warning receivers, followed by an external EW pod. The latter was not popular with Weasel crews since it occupied a valuable hardpoint and tended to interfere with the aircraft's sensors.

Two new weapons promised to tilt the balance: a new missile and a new model of Thunderchief. First into action was the missile, the General Dynamics AGM-78 Standard. Based on a proven naval SAM, this was intended to overcome some of the tactical limitations of the AGM-45.

As originally planned, the new Wild Weasel aircraft deployed as the main Standard ARM carrier should have been a version of the F-4 Phantom.

Right: The longer range and heavier warhead of the AGM-78 Standard anti-radiation missile greatly increased the combat effectiveness of the F-105G.

Left: The low-drag ALQ-105 electronic-warfare blisters on the sides of the F-105G fuselage were created by repackaging the systems from the ALQ-101 jamming pod.

Unfortunately for the USAF, the Wild Weasel 4 effort had become bogged down with technical problems. As McDonnell Douglas struggled to get the Weasel avionics working in a Phantom (a process which was eventually to stretch into 1968), it became obvious that the only way to get a better aircraft into the field urgently would be to develop another variant of the F-105F.

Development of what would become the F-150G Thunderchief (the designation had previously been used for the 1962 proposal for an improved two-seat aircraft) had started in the autumn of 1967. In place of the APR-25 and -26, this aircraft would have the new APR-35, -36 and -37. The APR-35 replaced the ER-142 panoramic receiver, while another earlier item of hardware — the QRC-317A (ALR-31) superheterodyne receiver — was replaced by the older SEE-SAMS. By dividing the internal systems of the ALQ-101 jamming pod between two fairings mounted on either side of the fuselage, Westinghouse created the ALQ-105 self-protection jammer. This could be used to protect the F-105G, but did not take up a valuable hardpoint.

The main missile armament of the F-105G would be the new and more effective AGM-78B version of the Standard ARM. Production of the -78B started in 1968 and swiftly superseded the interim A models. The -78B (Mod 1) could be fitted with two alternative patterns of seeker, both developed by Maxson. One covered E and G bands (2-3GHz and 6GHz), the other covering I-band (8-10GHz). The improved seeker on the AGM-78B-2 covered all three bands.

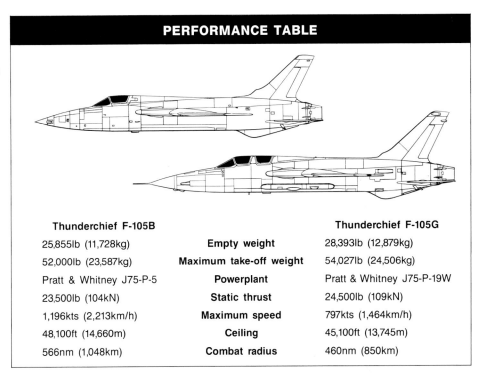

PERFORMANCE TABLE

Thunderchief F-105B		Thunderchief F-105G
25,855lb (11,728kg)	Empty weight	28,393lb (12,879kg)
52,000lb (23,587kg)	Maximum take-off weight	54,027lb (24,506kg)
Pratt & Whitney J75-P-5	Powerplant	Pratt & Whitney J75-P-19W
23,500lb (104kN)	Static thrust	24,500lb (109kN)
1,196kts (2,213km/h)	Maximum speed	797kts (1,464km/h)
48,100ft (14,660m)	Ceiling	45,100ft (13,745m)
566nm (1,048km)	Combat radius	460nm (850km)

Below: By the time of the Vietnam War ceasefire in January 1973, F-105Gs such as '265' of the 561st TFS had won the battle against North Vietnamese SAM sites.

Bottom: The sharks-mouth markings carried by 17th Wild Weasel Squadron were to be retained as the F-105G served on with the USAFE and the ANG.

Combat

PHASING-OUT

Seizure of the US Navy elint ship *Pueblo* by North Korea on 23 January 1968 triggered off further F-105 deployments to the Far East with six F-105 Wild Weasels from the Nellis-based 4525th Fighter Weapons Wing despatched to Osan Air Base, Korea, on 28 January 1968. The action was very much against the trend, however.

By March 1968, all Wild Weasel 3 (EF-105F) rebuilds had been completed. All F-105Fs reworked as Wild Weasels from now on would be to the F-105G standard. Some 12 F-105Gs from TAC's 23rd TFW at McConnell AFB left for Korat, Thailand, in April 1968 as part of Constant Guard I, one of several USAF deployments to the area that spring. The F-105F and G could be at best be interim systems, given that production of the F-105 had ended in 1964. In practice, they were to serve as the main operational Wild Weasels throughout the Vietnam War.

In August 1968, one of the 338th TFW's aircraft became the first Thunderchief to clock up 3,000 flying hours. By that time the aircraft had survived more than 500 missions and suffered battle damage and the effects of an air-to-air collision. By this time, the maximum number of aircraft in an F-105 squadron was being reduced from 21 to 18 and some squadrons had begun trading in their ''Thuds'' for Phantoms.

On 1 November 1968 President Johnson ordered a halt to the bombing campaign against North Vietnam; Rolling Thunder was over. It wasn't the end of the air war, however. Although responsibility for the ground

Right: 34th TFS F-105D carry what became a classic Vietnam War armament for the Thunderchief — six 750lb (340kg) bombs on the centreline, plus external tanks and EW pod.

war was being shifted to the South Vietnamese, US aicraft were still required to fly support missions over those areas in which North Vietnamese forces were operating.

The total Thunderchief losses for the year in South East Asia were 34 in combat and 12 through other causes. Later that month, the first F-4Es arrived in the theatre. By November 1968 work had started on modifying a batch of 16 EF-105Fs to

Above: With the Vietnam War hotting up following the North Vietnamese invasion of the South, 23rd TFW F-105G fly a training mission from McConnell AFB.

carry the more effective AGM-78B version of Standard. By June 1969 all 16 had been upgraded, and three months later the same weapon was selected for use on the F-105G. The -78C, -78D and 78D-2 followed in

Above: A group of 35th TFW F-105s being delivered to the ANG in 1980. The dorsal spine on aircraft 490 (tailcode TH) is the Thunderstick II upgrade.

1969, 1970 and 1971 respectively. These carried new types of seeker developed by Bendix or General Dynamics, and modified fuzing systems and rocket motors.

In September 1969 flight trials of the long-awaited improved nav/attack system finally started at Eglin AFB. The Thunderstick II/LORAN suite was now based on ITT's ARN-92 LORAN system and introduced a prominent dorsal spine on the modified aircraft. A batch of 30 F-105Ds was converted to the Thunderstick II standard, the first becoming operational in the USA in March 1970.

The combat losses for 1969

Right: The "Thud" needed long runways, and the assistance of a braking parachute on landing. This aircraft is touching down at U-Tapao in southern Thailand.

amounted to only 14 Thunderchiefs, obviously due to decreased activity and numbers.

Deliveries of Wild Weasel Phantoms had started that year with the modified aircraft serving with the 81st TFW, at Spangdahlem AB in West Germany, and the 67th TFS, at Kadena AB in Okinawa. The designation EF-4C applied to these aircraft seems to have been unofficial. The 81st introduced USAFE to Wild Weasel operations,

but at first there was no combat role for the 67th.

By early 1970, some of the F-105Ds in Thailand had passed the 3,500 hour mark and retirement from combat could not be long delayed. That retirement was being forced not by obsolescence, but by attrition. The Thunderchief was still faster than any other USAF type when loaded with 12 750lb (340kg) bombs.

In October of that year, the 355th

Combat

TFW and its F-105s began to redeploy back to the USA and the unit was deactivated in December, its aircraft being passed to two 23rd TFW training squadrons. Now only the Wild Weasels were left in action out of the original Thunderchief force.

In November, two Air National Guard (ANG) units were ordered to convert to the Republic aircraft. January of the following year saw the first F-105Ds reaching the 184th Tactical Fighter Training Group at McConnell AFB and the 192nd Tactical Fighter Group at Byrd Field, Virginia. A third ANG unit, the 113rd TFG at Andrews AFB Maryland, was also re-equipped.

Late in July, modification of the last of the batch of 30 Thunderstick II F-105Ds was finally completed. These aircraft served only with the 457th TFS, a unit tasked with the precision-bombing role. No more were converted to the Thunderstick II standard.

USAF plans called for the delivery of 60 F-105Gs, and a growing shortage of F-105Fs available for conversion forced the USAF to hunt for suitable

aircraft. The summer of 1971 saw six Combat Martin and six Commando Nail Thunderchiefs stripped of their specialized systems and rebuilt as F-105Gs. The final number built was 61: two prototypes, followed by a first batch of 49 production aircraft, then a second batch of 12. The end was drawing ever near for the F-105.

Below: A Wild Weasel from the 561st TFS flies a Shrike mission in October 1972. A shortage of Weasels forced the USAF to hunt for convertible two-seaters.

LINEBACKER I AND II

By the spring of 1972, only 15 USAF tactical squadrons were in South East Asia, little more than a third of the peak deployment of 41 in 1968. As the situation in Vietnam deteriorated, President Nixon ordered more USAF aircraft to be despatched to the area. On the night of 30 March North Vietnamese forces invaded South Vietnam with three divisions pushing south until driven back in mid-May by US and South Vietnamese intensive counter-attacking.

Left: January 1973 and as North Vietnam finally starts serious peace negotiations, the war is almost over for ''Thuds'' such as this 561st TFS Wild Weasel.

An early part of the US counter-attack was an order by President Nixon on 6 May to mount air raids into North Vietnam as far north as the 20th parallel. Two days later the Linebacker I air raids began with US aircraft flying the sort of no-holds-barred missions which should have been carried out back in 1965. By now only a single squadron of F-105Gs was left at Korat, but a dozen F-105Gs from the 561st TFS at McConnell AFB left the US on 7 April to join the build-up of forces. Arriving at Korat on 12 April, they were in action the same day.

At the opening of Linebacker I, the NVAF had around 250 MiGs, a third of which were MiG-21s. These were supplemented by nearly 300 SAM sites and more than 1,500 anti-aircraft guns. Coping with this threat required the best of US technology, including

Below: By March 1984 Hill AFB had only a single F-105D. This veteran serves in the final role of some ageing Thunderchiefs, that of ''gate guardian''.

the F-105G and its Standard missiles. Chaff, EW, Wild Weasels, and large numbers of F-4 Phantoms were the ingredients in a campaign which won and maintained air-superiority over the skies of North Vietnam.

Linebacker I lasted until 22 October, when bombing north of the 20th parallel was suspended in order to encourage peace talks in Paris. At first, an agreement seemed likely in November and air operations over all but the most southern part of North Vietnam were halted.

THE F-105's FINAL FLING

Several USAF Reseve units switched from the transport to the strike role in 1972, with F-105Ds being issued to the 507th TFG at Tinker AFB in June, and to the 301st Tactical Fighter Wing at Carswell AFB, Texas, in August.

Even the elderly F-105B was used in this re-equipment programme, with the 508th TFW at Hill AFB receiving the older aircraft. The latter had long since left USAF service; the 508th's ''new'' mounts came from the 177th TFG, a New Jersey ANG unit which was being converted to the F-106 Delta Dart.

As the Vietnam peace talks dragged fruitlessly on, the 67th TFS at Okinawa was also assigned to Korat, arriving there in time for its Wild

Above: One of the surviving F-105B-6REs was still operational with the Air Force Reserve's 466th TFS at Hill AFB when this photo was taken in 1977.

Weasel Phantoms to participate in the Linebacker II raids which started on the night of 22 December. The new aircraft helped supplement the anti-radar capability of the surviving F-105Gs.

The goal of Linebacker II was to apply the full weight of US air power, including the first B-52 missions against Hanoi. As the huge bombers flew through the darkness night after night, F-105Gs and chaff-laying aircraft flew ahead of them. After 606 tactical strikes involving 729 B-52 sorties, plus more than 2,000 by fighters and other strike aircraft, the bombing was suspended on 29 December. Total US losses had been only three per cent of the total force launched against the most sophisticated air defences ever tested in battle. By early January, the skies of North Vietnam had been cleared of MiGs and SAMs.

Linebacker II was successful in forcing the North Vietnamese to begin serious negotiations to end the war. A ceasefire agreement was signed in Paris on 23 January 1973. Five days later, the ceasefire took effect. For the United States, the war was finally over.

FOLLOWING the ceasefire on 28 January 1973 which temporarily ended the war, most F-105Gs were pulled back to the USA. Evidence for the timescale of this retirement is contradictory. According to an official USAF history published in 1978, by the summer of 1973 the USAF would have only six F-105Ds left in its inventory. Four were used as trainers, the remaining two as trials aircraft. Combat attrition plus the F-105G rebuild programme had thinned the ranks of the F-105F fleet, with only 17 still flying — five with the USAF and eight with the ANG.

Unfortunately for this neat official view, the Thunderchief seems to have ignored the history book. Many authorities on the Republic aircraft agree that the last F-105G left Thailand at the end of October 1974, nine years after the first Thunderchiefs had deployed to that country. Back in the USA, the 35th TFW at Georgia AFB had been operating F-105Gs since 1973, and would operate two squadrons of these Wild Weasels until the arrival of the follow-on F-4G in the late 1970s.

Early 1975 saw a steady deterioration in South Vietnamese military capability, which ended as a disastrous retreat from the northern part of the country in April 1975. On 29 April came, what was for US military aviation, the last act of the war: Operation Frequent Wind, the helicopter evacuation of Saigon.

As a procession of helicopters

Right: The smog on the horizon shows that this is not Vietnam but the USA. A maintained F-105G Weasel spends its twilight years with the Georgia ANG.

wound its way again and again from the ships offshore to the roof of the US embassy, the skies above them were guarded by US combat aircraft, including the then-new Grumman F-14 Tomcat. At least one source claims that an older warplane was also in the skies over Saigon that day — a handful of elderly F-105Gs flying from Korat for the last time.

Fact or legend? The truth is buried in USAF archives for future historians to uncover. If the last war-weary "Thuds" were in action that day, no warplane has earned to right to be there more than Republic's F-105. Since the Vietnam war had begun for the USAF, 321 had been lost in combat and a further 62 from other causes — slightly more than half of all the D and F models which had rolled off the Republic production line.

With the Vietnam War finally over, time started to run out for the surviving Thunderchiefs. As newer fighters such as the F-15 and F-16 entered service in growing numbers, large

numbers of F-4 Phantoms were available to replace the Republic warplane.

Unlike many classic USAF fighters of the past, the F-105 never saw foreign service, either in the shape of export orders or ex-USAF "hand-me-downs". Attempts were made in the summer of 1960 to sell the F-105D to Britain and France and presentations were made to the air forces of both nations. The proposed French version would have retained the J75 engine, but the UK was offered the option of using the Bristol Olympus BO1.22R, the massive 31,000lb (14,000kg) thrust engine already being developed for the English Electric TSR.2 strike aircraft.

Both nations were offered local production rights, but the entire idea of a European F-105D fell on largely-deaf ears. French industry was already developing two Mach 2 designs: the Mirage III fighter and the Mirage IV bomber; while in Britain the RAF and industry were firmly wedded to the TSR.2 of their own.

Plans in the early 1960s to develop advanced versions of the F-105 were equally unsuccessful. Two proposed variants were the F-105G and F-105H. Based on the D model, the F-105G would have had the 31in (79cm) fuselage stretch of the new F model, and been powered by the Pratt & Whitney B-24 engine, a 30,000lb (13,600kg) thrust version of the J75. Extra fuel would have been packed into a dorsal spine and tanks in the fuselage sides, and the landing gear strengthened to cope with the higher all-up weight. The USAF declined to order the aircraft either as new-build, or as a rework of the F-105D fleet. Although the project was shelved, the designation was re-used in 1970 for the F-105G Wild Weasel anti-radar aircraft.

The F-105H concept was equally unsucccessful. Based on the two-seat -F model, it would have combined the new engine of the -G with a larger wing, horizontal tail surfaces, an enlarged vertical fin (or a MiG-23-style retractable ventral fin), and a new tandem-wheel under-carriage.

With the arrival of its F-4G Wild Weasels in 1978, the 35th TFW was able to retire its ageing F-105Gs; but there was life in the old girl yet. Some went into storage at Davis-Monthan AFB in Arizona, but the lucky ones were issued to the 128th TFS of the 116th TFW, Georgia ANG. Conversion started on 1 January 1979 and five of the unit's aircraft deployed to Nellis AFB in March for a Red Flag exercise.

Other ANG and Air Force Reserve units re-equipped with the Thunderchief, but age was beginning to tell on

Right: By the late-1970s F-105 Thunderchiefs were becoming difficult to maintain but hardworking ground crew kept some in service until 1983.

Above: 23rd TFW Thunderchiefs fly to a new role with the Air Force Reserve in April 1972. Some would serve for another decade before finally being paid off.

these surviving F-105s. From mid-1980 onwards, a catalogue of technical problems began to mount up: faulty fuel cells, cracks in the main landing gear side braces, engine combustion chamber cases, and even wing spars. Many replacement components salvaged from Davis Monthan were equally defectve. The Georgia ANG adopted a "Can Do" attitude with the number of flyable aircraft rising from an all-time low of three to half their total fleet of 12; and they even devised a scheme which allowed the carriage of a Standard ARM on the centreline.

Despite such efforts, the end of the line for the war-weary "Thuds" could not be long delayed. By the spring of 1982 most of the Thunderstick I aircraft had been retired and the 466th TFS was the last surviving F-105 unit. On 25 May 1983 an F-105 of the Georgia ANG flew the unit's final official F-105 mission. Lettering on the underwing fuel tanks said it all: "THUDS FOREVER".

INDEX